H. KHATUN

PRICELESS
PUBLICITY

how to get
MONEY-CAN'T-BUY
media coverage
for your business

A HAYAT HOUSE book

First published in Great Britain in 2022 by Hayat House.

Copyright © Hayat House 2022

The moral right of Halima Khatun to be identified as the author of this work has been asserted by her in accordance with the Copyright, Design and Patents Act, 1988.

Cover design by Felix Diaz de Escauriaza

Table of Contents

Priceless Publicity 1

Introduction 2

Getting the most out of this book.................................... 5

Demystifying PR 8

Good vs. bad PR 17

Demystifying the media 24

The mind of a journalist 25

What makes the news? 31

Campaigns 36

Research... 39

Product or service launch... 42

Business development.. 45

Awards... 47

Thought leadership 49

The right stories for the right media............................... 52

National examples 58

Right stories - Regional 64

Regional examples 68

Right stories – Trade... 75

Trade examples.. 84

Right stories – Online 88

Online examples 92

Etiquette 97

Finding the story in your business................................. 102

The key questions to ask yourself 103

News story or a non-story... 109

Press release example - Elliot for Water.......................... 114

Press release example: RBE.. 135

Press release 101 148

Press release tips and tricks 155
Emailing your press release 160
Pitching...163
Could it be simpler?..168
Case study interview - Ruth Rees......................................172
Turbo-charging your PR with case studies.......................174
Final note..183
Was this book helpful? If so, please leave a review!........184

Priceless Publicity

Introduction

I'm going to keep this short and sweet, because I know you want to get to the good stuff. There's nothing worse than an author telling you their life story as an introduction.

However, I am including a bit about myself because I think it's really important, in the sea of self-appointed gurus, to know that I know my stuff.

I always knew I wanted to write. After completing a degree in English and Marketing and then studying Broadcast Journalism as a postgraduate, I began a career as a TV and radio news reporter, freelancing for ITV, the BBC and independent stations.

However, this career was short-lived, because I quickly realised it was less about writing, and more about camera angles, pictures, editing and constant deadlines.

I remember the moment I decided it wasn't for me. A 14-year-old girl had been hit by a train, and as a reporter it was my job to doorstep her neighbours and mourning family, hoping to get an interview, the day after her death.

I then moved to the dark side, otherwise known as public relations, or PR. I worked for one of the largest PR groups in the country, juggling multiple clients, before going in-house and specialising in healthcare PR. The best bit about the job? It was all about storytelling.

I'd interview people from all walks of life, find out their stories and get them out to the media. I generated coverage in national newspapers and magazines, as well as TV and radio.

After nearly a decade in the industry, I decided to go it alone, setting up my own PR consultancy, where I got to work with a host of clients from business coaches, to stress specialists, and even an aviation recruitment firm.

I noticed a gap in the market, where the small businesses were missing out on media coverage because they didn't have the deep pockets to hire a PR consultancy. Or worse still, they spent a lot of money on a PR agent but didn't feel like they got the return they wanted.

I knew there was a solution to this, enabling and empowering these amazing small businesses to do their own PR, to know what a good story looks like and to have the confidence to pick up the phone and speak to a journalist.

I started doing training sessions, teaching the skills I learned to small business owners. It was an amazing, rewarding experience and, to this day, I consult privately.

But here is the exciting bit... and the bit that's perhaps most relevant to you. After the birth of my children, I took a step back from my career, worked less and fulfilled my other childhood dream - I wrote a novel. My book, *The Secret Diary of an Arranged Marriage*, spawned a series and won awards. Best of all, courtesy of having a background in PR and journalism, I managed to generate money can't buy publicity for my book in the likes of Good Housekeeping, the Metro, and the BBC. Alongside this, I wrote a lifestyle blog, for which I generated lots of media coverage, too.

You can see examples on my respective press pages:
Author site: https://halimakhatun.co.uk/in-the-press/
Blog: https://www.halimabobs.com/in-the-press

I have done PR for clients in numerous sectors, from aviation, to healthcare to property and construction, from big corporates to sole traders and my own author business and blog. I hope this shows that with the help of the teachings in this book, you really can generate amazing publicity for whatever business you have.

What is in this book is your ticket to priceless publicity that your business truly deserves.

Getting the most out of this book

You've just made the best decision for your business.

Congratulations on taking the first step towards giving your business the credibility, publicity and awareness that it truly deserves. Also, well done on saving yourself a tonne of money on hiring a PR consultant, or worse, not doing anything at all, and seeing your competitors getting great publicity.

By reading and implementing the teachings of this book, you will gift your business the greatest chance of growth and success by making sure that the people *you* want to know about your business know:

- Who you are.

- What you do.

- You are the go-to person in your sector.

This PR book is your manual. It's a PR expert in your pocket. On tap. At your service at all times. Okay, I'll stop now because I think you get the picture.

What to expect

I broke the book down into different sections and I'm going to walk you through all of it, step-by-step, because there is a LOT to take in. There's no fluff or vague information here. It's a deep-dive. Below are just some things we'll cover:

- What is PR?

- What it can do for your business.

- How to deal with journalists.

- How to find a story in your business.

- How to secure amazing publicity that money cannot buy.

As there's a lot to digest, I recommend you read this book at your own pace, take breaks, drink coffee, and make notes. It's your PR companion and will be here for you to revisit as and when you need to.

A couple of things to bear in mind...

First, what you put in is what you will get out. By engaging through the modules, taking the learning and expertise and, crucially, applying it all, will mean that you give yourself the best chance of PR success.

Second, ignore those voices in your head that are saying:

- *My business isn't interesting enough to be featured in the media.*

- *I've never spoken to a journalist.*

- *I don't have time for this.*

- *This is a bit intimidating. I won't be able to do this.*

I am telling you now, without any hesitation, that your business IS interesting enough and you can do this. As for the not talking to journalists bit, don't worry. I've got you covered with a whole section.

The beauty of this book is you don't need to be a PR expert. It's made for you if you know nothing about PR. I will talk you through every single element.

Regarding the time bit, getting good PR for your business shouldn't be so labour intensive that you can't get on with the day job of building and running your own business. You won't turn into a PR consultant. You will be able to read this book in your own time, around your day job and learn how to apply PR to your business because, ultimately, that's what matters.

So keep reading, as this will be the best investment you've made for your business.

Demystifying PR

What is PR?

You may have heard the letters P and R thrown about. You may have a vague understanding of what it is. It may conjure up certain connotations and depictions you've seen on TV or films. Or you might not have a clue what it means.

There's no shame in the latter.

I've been working in the PR industry for over a decade and my closest family and friends still don't quite understand what I do.

So here's a basic 101:

One of the key definitions of PR, or public relations, is *the practice of working with the press (whether that's broadcast, print or online media) to raise awareness or influence public opinion about a particular person, organisation, issue or event.*

Essentially, the public are the target audience / end users and you're working with the media to get messages across to them.

I'm going to go into a lot more detail later but, as an example, if your target audience is other business owners, you might want to get yourself into business publications with thought leadership articles in order to be seen as an expert talking about business development.

The idea is that people will know about you and your brand and see that your shop, whether that's figurative or literal, is open for business.

Isn't PR the same as advertising?

Short answer: no.

I say to people that after doing my course or reading this book, they will never look at a newspaper, magazine or online outlet the same way again. And neither will you.

Put simply: Advertising is paid for. PR is free.

So the thing with advertising is that you pay, whether it's a few hundred or a few thousand pounds or dollars, for that space in the publication. The reader knows it's been paid for, too. They'll know that you paid the salesperson to put that ad in the paper and to write those words about you.

Here are some examples of the adverts you might gloss over every day:

- An author's new book release.

- A doggy training business with an advert that goes along the lines of: "Available for doggy training in Manchester. Best in town."

- A furniture store with a 20% discount for new customers.

- A restaurant that's opened in your area.

- A family run law firm specialising in wills and probate, priding themselves on their personalised service.

The advert might be in a different colour to stand out from the page. It might have pictures. It may contain graphics. It will always, always, highlight the company being advertised in the best light.

If you've ever opened a newspaper or looked on a news site, you'll spot the difference between an advert and a news story.

And what does that mean? It means the reader will know it's biased. They'll know it's pay for play. So unless it's something they need at exactly that moment, they'll likely gloss over it.

No business ever bad-mouthed themselves in an advert.

This is perhaps the simplest way of summarising an advert. It's a promotional piece about a business. There is nothing wrong with this and adverts certainly have their place. However, PR is completely different.

PR is not paid for in cash, it's paid for in credibility. You've earned that spot in the media because you're working with the journalist to give them a story that's interesting and relevant enough for them to place in their publication.

The beauty of this (and where the real magic of PR comes in) is that as a reader, you don't know that a PR person, or a PR-savvy business owner, has pitched the story to a journalist. You'll just see it as a regular story. You'll stop. You'll read it. You'll take interest. And that may lead to sales.

I would urge you to go and look at your local newspaper, or an online magazine after this chapter, because you'll see a lot of stories have been pitched by a PR person or business owner. The rest may be the usual stories that dictate the news agenda, for example, something that's happened in the area such as a crime or a flood. These are the stories that a journalist has sought out. However, the majority are brought together by PR people putting relevant stories to journalists, while simultaneously highlighting the business, product, or service that they are promoting.

There's a key word there: relevant. In order for a story to be featured, it has to be relevant to the publication that the journalist is writing for. If you can figure out that bit - what stories work for the publications you'd like to be featured in - you greatly increase your chance of being featured.

That is exactly what this book teaches you. How to pitch *your* stories of relevance (and don't worry, I'm going to tell you what kind of stories work and crucially, what are the stories within your business) that journalists will want to hear. We just need to find them.

How PR works

You give the story to the journalist and they decide whether it merits a place in their publication. Again, don't worry, I'll be talking you through exactly how you 'give' the story to a journalist, complete with done-for-you templates.

However, before I dive into that, I want to talk a little about what good PR can do for you.

I'm guessing that, as you've bought this book, you already see the value in PR but even so, you might have heard the word bandied around but you might not fully understand how to apply it to your business and reap the benefits.

Good PR does a number of things that are hugely beneficial. Below are some examples...

It can raise your profile

Quite simply, if you're in a particular publication, people read about you, people hear about you, people know about you.

It's a really basic rule of business - if people don't know about you, how are they going to buy your product or service? How will they know to come to you? How will they know you're available? On a very basic level, PR provides brand awareness, without having to spend a lot of money on advertising.

It can boost your credibility

I've already mentioned this but it's worth saying again. PR is *earned* media coverage. You can look at an advert with an air of cynicism and say: "Well, of course they're going to say they've got the best sofas in the world," or "of course they're going to say they've got the best business consultancy," or "obviously they're going to say they're the go-to for events and conferences," because they've paid for that spot in the publication.

Whereas PR is not paid for. It's earned its place in the publication on its own merit, because the story was good enough to be featured. So you read it without that level of cynicism.

There's a general PR industry rule that an article's value is three times more than the cost of an advert in the same publication. For example, if a half-page advert in a regional newspaper costs £1,500, the value of an article of the equivalent size in the same publication is £4,500. This may seem arbitrary but the thinking is that an article that sits within the context of the other stories in that publication is more likely to be taken as read and trusted, therefore more powerful as a marketing tool.

Also, being featured in a publication for good news about your business (and we'll talk later about all the forms of good news there are) will mean that by default you'll be seen as an expert in your field, by default you've got credibility, and by default the reader will think your business must be an authority in what it does. This then plants a seed in the reader's mind - they will come to YOU when they need your service.

It can help with your website SEO

When I first started out in PR and mentioned SEO to my clients, it was greeted with a blank face.

However, in this increasingly digitised world, more and more businesses are aware of the need to have a strong online presence.

As you know, customers will come to you in a number of ways. If you're a business coach, you might meet potential clients at a networking event. If you're an author, potential readers may come across your work through a recommendation. If you're a blogger or influencer, your entire business is built online.

Whatever you do for a living, potential customers usually do their homework. And they do this via the web. They'll check out your website, read reviews on trusted sites, see what presence you have on social media.

If they go on your website and see that you've got a media page where you show you've been featured on news sites like The Daily Mail, or whatever your target publication is, it gives you a huge credibility boost.

Also, having your business featured in different, authoritative media publications, such as the BBC or a local news site, boosts your SEO. Having your name and your business name in various publications that Google recognises as authorities helps your website rise in the online rankings, which ultimately will make it easier for your ideal customers to find you. There is a running joke that goes along the lines of-if you want to hide a dead body, the best place is on page 3 of Google, because no one ever looks there. Getting your business name and web link on reputable websites increases your chance of hitting the first page of Google, therefore increasing your discoverability.

It can boost your algorithm

In a social-media dominated marketplace, you can showcase any PR coverage on all your social platforms, tagging the publications that featured you, which will not only provide great content, it'll get more eyeballs on your socials, too.

It can turbo charge your marketing

If you get into different publications, you can use this in your marketing literature. It makes for a great 'as featured in' section on any flyer, or even an email signature, and instantly adds gravitas.

As you can see, the opportunities are vast in terms of what good PR can do for you.

While there are many types of PR which require different approaches (I've got you covered on that, too), the end results are the same:

- There should be an increase in enquiries to your business.

- An increase in ROI (return on investment) for the time you spend on PR.

- The growth of your brand.

- A growth in revenue.

As I've said, the more people know about you, the greater the chances of people buying your product or services, which will lead to overall business growth.

Something to remember (I have to throw in a caveat) - PR is a drip-drip process. Results won't be achieved overnight.

For example, the journalist might not take one story you pitch, such as a business milestone or store opening but they might accept another article you put forward, such as a new product launch.

Or, you might get a great piece of coverage but the phone might not ring off the hook straight away. You shouldn't be disheartened by that because it takes time to build brand recognition and for PR to make an impact.

Think about it this way - when you do your business projections, you don't think: *Okay, I'm going to give it a few months and if it doesn't work out, I'm going to do something else.*

You'll have a long-term vision and PR should sit nicely within your plans because it's an investment in your business development and over time (and that time could be a few weeks or a few months), you should see greater brand awareness, which will lead to more customers.

The beauty of reading this book is, rather than investing in a consultant to do your PR over a fixed period of 12-18 months or more, you're actually taking the learnings and doing it yourself at your own pace. As a financial investment, it's a very affordable one-off. Time-wise, the investment is higher, as you'll need to action your learnings, but the returns should be much greater.

Another point to mention (which I'm going to spend quite a bit of time on throughout this book as it's so important) is that just because something matters to you, it doesn't necessarily mean it's going to be hold-the-front-page news for a journalist. I've had many a conversation with a healthcare PR client politely explaining that meeting the bare minimum standards for infection rates isn't news, it's what people would expect. Or telling a private corporate client how their jargon-laden mission statement would not pique the interest of a local news reporter. I'm going to teach you how to ruthlessly unpick the stories so the journalists you are targeting get the best news from you, which will in turn increase your chances of scoring some great media coverage. In fact, we're going to walk through this in the next chapter.

Good vs. bad PR

So now we're going to talk about good PR versus bad PR.

You might be thinking: *Is this relevant to me? I just want to learn about good PR.*

However, I'm including this because when I've been doing in-person masterclasses, I've found that a lot of businesses get approached by PR agencies who have offered to do their publicity, get them in various publications and build their brand.

It sounds great but business owners have shared the same concern - they don't know what they don't know. They don't know what is good PR or what they should be getting for their money. Everything they're hearing from the agency sounds amazing but it's a little smoke and mirrors.

I recently did a talk with start-ups and many said that they had their fingers burnt, where they paid a good amount of money to a PR agency and, as the months went by and the invoices ran into tens of thousands of pounds, these start-ups found they weren't getting the coverage they wanted. They didn't know what they initially bought into, and the result was a gap between their expectation and the agency's delivery. So that's what this section focuses on - what a good PR service looks like.

Knowing what to expect from PR agencies

It might not be relevant for you right now, however, there may come a point when you don't have enough time to spend on your own PR and will need to outsource it.

You might be surprised to hear a lot of people that do my PR course and read my book have said they want to learn all about the discipline, learn how to find a story, how to engage with journalists, etc. but not so they can do their own PR - they want to learn so they can commission the right agency to do it for them. These business owners want to learn everything so they know what they're getting for their money.

Walking the walk

I've worked in the PR industry for over a decade. I started out as a broadcast journalist, so I like to think I can walk the walk as well as talk a good PR game.

I personally feel it really helps to be able to pitch a story when you've been on the other side and you know what stories you'd take as a journalist and what kind of angles would work for a publication.

I'm in a quite unique position in that I've worked for the public sector, the private sector and the third (or charity) sector, so I've got a broad view, as opposed to PR professionals who are in one sector or have certain specialisms.

This may sound like I'm tooting my own horn but the reason I'm sharing this is because due to my experience as a journalist, then a multi-sector PR consultant who has hired other agencies as well as been hired, I'm in a good position to share what good and bad PR looks like. I've seen it all.

Let's start with the good...

Being a great storyteller

You're going to see a theme in this book, and that is how much I talk about the importance of storytelling.

You want your PR person to really get under the skin of your story, to really understand your brand and find out what your passions are and why you are where you are in your business.

No one wakes up in the morning and says: "I'm going to start a dog training business," or "I'm going to be an author," or "I'm going set up a yoga studio." These things aren't decided on a whim. Usually, it comes from a passion, so you want your PR person to be excited about that and to get fired up about your story and find different angles for your business. They need to take your business goals, aims and ambitions and turn them into stories that the media will want to hear.

I am a huge believer in having a solid understanding of good storytelling as a core principle of PR. This might sound like a no-brainer but, believe it or not, you do get situations where you speak to a PR person and they don't necessarily know the storytelling fundamentals, because they've been trained a certain way.

Can PR any sector

A good PR person can do PR for any business in any sector. They may specialise and focus on a particular area, however, they should have the basic principles, which I learned in journalism school. The main principle is to really, truly know what makes a good story. And they should be able to find that good story in *your* business.

Whether you've got a fashion line, a book business, a blog, or a consultancy service, the ability to recognise a good story is a skill you will need to get yourself into any publication, and that's exactly what you should expect from a PR consultancy.

A background in journalism

I've already said this but it's worth more detail. When you've worn that hat, you understand:

- The challenges journalists face.
- Why it's sometimes difficult to engage them and how you get around that.

Another plus of hiring a PR person with a background in journalism is that they bring their newshound skills to the table. They can produce print-ready copy and print-ready press releases. I'll often write a press release or article for a client and it'll get printed word-for-word on a news site. I could say it's because I'm an amazing writer, but most likely it's a combination of writing well and writing how a journalist wants a story to be published.

These days, journalists are so short on time (which I'll go into later on) that they want print-ready stories on a plate. So knowing how to write like a journalist is a huge plus.

Now let's look at some of the bad PR practices.

Relying solely on media contacts

I'm quite different in saying this, as the PR industry in general prides itself on its contacts' book. However, a heavy contacts book does not constitute good PR. Here's why...

I studied broadcast journalism and a lot of my classmates went on to great places like the BBC, CNN, ITN and Good Morning America. Many others worked for national and regional newspapers, magazines and radio stations. However, just because they're my friends, it doesn't mean they'll print or broadcast my story. For example, I spent a lot of time in private healthcare PR and one of my good friends was a BBC health reporter, so you'd assume I had a guaranteed ear for my stories, right? Wrong. He was covering major stories, like global pandemics, or NHS staff shortages. My stories about my private sector employer were not what he was looking for. He wanted world firsts. Major medical breakthroughs. I didn't have that, so having a contact in such a great news organisation didn't give me any advantage.

The flip side is this: you, as a business owner, won't have media contacts. The great news is, because I'm going to teach you about the principles of journalism, the reliance on media contacts will be unnecessary, because your stories will be good enough.

Later on in this book, I'm going to talk to you about how to find journalists and how to get their contacts and pitch to them successfully.

Blanket pitches everyone

No journalist wants to be blind copied into an email with a press release that they know has been sent to 300 other people. If it's not tailored to them, the chances of them reading it are a lot slimmer than if a PR person has addressed them directly and said: "*I've got a great story for you because of...*"

That's a much better pitch, as it shows that your PR consultant or agency is taking the time and representing your brand in the best light, whereas if it's a blanket, catch-all email, the chances of getting lost in the journalist's inbox (which can run up to hundreds of emails a day) is pretty high.

Treats you like just a number

Unfortunately, a lot of small businesses have fallen victim to being just a number on a PR consultant's portfolio. I remember a tech start-up that splashed out on PR support after getting a round of investment funding. They were feeling flush and went for the biggest agency they could afford, the one with the most impressive client list.

Unfortunately, the more you pay, the bigger a client you are and the more care and attention you receive. That's just how it works, which meant this start-up, with its relatively modest retainer, was never top priority. There was a disconnect between what the start-up expected from the agency, and what the agency was willing to provide. However, a good PR agency or consultant will give you due care and attention and you shouldn't feel like just a number. You should feel like you are getting value for money.

You may be thinking, how would you know what value looks like? Well, luckily for you, you're reading this book and by the end of it, you'll not only know how to generate amazing results driven PR, you'll know exactly what good PR looks like should you ever want, or need, to outsource in the future.

Demystifying the media

This section is all about journalists, because everything you've read so far - what PR is, what it can do for you, good and bad PR - will only make sense when you know about how journalists operate and how PR and journalism go hand in hand.

I'm going to cover the whole gambit because it's important for you to understand the different types of journalists out there and how they operate, so you can position your business towards what they need, and provide stories that they will feature.

Whatever business you're in, you *will* have great stories the media will want to hear. It's about finding the stories and finding the journalists that would be interested in those stories. Then you bring the two together with a pitch or press release, which will result in amazing coverage.

Sounds good? I'm glad to hear it.

Now, this section is quite intensive as I'm going to cover a lot of ground. Feel free to pause, take your time to go through it all and make lots of notes. There will be plenty of practical examples, which means it's not just me waxing lyrical. You actually have some context as to where this all fits in.

So let's get started...

The mind of a journalist

You might think: *why do I need to understand a journalist? I'm busy enough learning about PR!*

Simply put, without journalists, there is no PR.

Think about it this way - imagine your ideal customer. In order to encourage them to buy your product or service, you'd need to know more about them. What motivates them? What interests them? What's their need that your business can fill? A journalist is exactly the same, because they are your client in a sense, or certainly your stakeholder, because they are the ones that can be the enabler - or the barrier - between you and great coverage. Therefore, knowing how journalists operate and how they think will really help you understand how to pitch to them appropriately.

Once you can unlock the thinking of a journalist, everything else in this book, such as how to pitch, when to pitch, etc. will all come together.

In the mind of a journalist

I'm going to talk in general terms here, but most journalists are...

Underpaid

This isn't a boohoo, pity-all-journalists ploy. It's a cold hard truth of the occupation. I started out as a journalist. Trust me, they are very underpaid.

Most people go into journalism because they love writing. It's never for the money.

You will understand why I'm telling you this as you read on, but essentially you really do have to cut to the chase with them.

Bombarded with PR stories

When I was a journalist working for a local radio station, I would get a couple of hundred stories in my inbox every day. Most were irrelevant, blanket emails which were clearly sent to many other journalists. I was at a radio station in Manchester and I would get local stories from Scotland, or I'd get a press release about a very niche topic that just didn't have a home on the local radio. It was as though the people sending these stories (whether they're PR consultants or business owners) didn't care about who they were pitching to. It was a numbers game for them. Send it to enough people and someone will bite. It was the equivalent of throwing mud at a wall and seeing what sticks. As a result, I would go on a mass-deleting spree to clear my inbox of these irrelevant stories, which meant that many a good story may have got lost in the culling. Because journalists are so heavily bombarded with press releases, it's even harder for good stories to come through. Therefore, you have to make sure your pitch is really tight and concise.

Overworked

Most journalists are always on a deadline and you'll find that the deadline is usually yesterday. If they work for a national paper they've got daily deadlines. If they're at a weekly publication they might have deadlines on a Thursday afternoon but they're working on it the whole week. If they're with an online publication, the poor journalist's deadline is constant. The emergence of 24-hour news means they can't beautifully craft stories because they simply do not have time. The golden days of journalists spending the whole day out in the community, having long lunches, meeting people, knocking on doors and finding stories are long gone. Nowadays, they need the stories to be brought to them. And that's where you can help.

When I worked in local radio, there could have been a fire across the street and I could not go and report on it because I had to deliver half-hourly news bulletins and couldn't leave my desk. I needed those emails, press releases and pitches from businesses. I needed the stories to come to me. That's the case for most journalists, they rely on good stories being sent by PR people or direct from business owners.

Straight from the horse's mouth

It's all well and good for me to use my anecdotal experience as a journalist to tell you how they operate and how this can work for you. However, I wanted to show you that this experience is across-the-board for all journalists. I spoke to some of my media contacts because I wanted to share with you how they feel when they're interacting and getting stories from PR agencies.

A digital editor of a regional business magazine said:

"We always consider whether the story has significance for the region's business community and specifically company owners, so

mergers and acquisitions activity, flotations, property transactions and administrations will always interest our readers. We don't write for consumers so we're not interested in businesses launching new products but we would be interested in the impact of those products on the business itself."

There are quite a few things you can take from that and you can bet your bottom dollar he still got plenty of product launches and consumer pitches sent to him every day, even though they were totally irrelevant. Don't be that person. Be better. Make sure you know what the publication wants. You can figure that out quite easily. And I'll tell you how...

All you need to do is **read the publication**.

I know that sounds patronising but, believe me, the number of times clients have said they want to get in publication x or y, and I'd ask: "Have you read that publication? Have you seen what stories they cover? Have you seen them covering stories similar to yours?"

Often, the answer is no to at least one of those questions. Often, it's a no to the first question.

Reading the publications you want to be featured in needn't be an onerous task. If you read just two to three stories, you can get a good idea of what that journalist and outlet writes about. In fact, I might set that as some homework for you at the end of this section.

A regional TV reporter said:

"To me, it's a tricky balance between deciding what is news and what is interesting. For example, a business taking on a lot of extra staff and helping the wider community is a prime example of a local business doing good and is a great story but quite often

businesses make the mistake of putting forward a story that is just an obvious promotional piece and that isn't newsworthy."

This is really important and is something I talked about earlier. Sometimes what's of interest to you might not be of interest to the journalist. Yes, you want to get your name out there, but not as a sell or a promotional piece. If you want them to word-for-word say: *This business is fantastic because we said so,* you have to pay for it. It's called advertising and it's expensive.

A national newspaper editor said:

"When I receive a press release from a business, I ask myself the following questions: 1) Is the story regarding a household name? 2) Is the story interesting enough for the public to care? Is it close to home i.e. a UK based story or a European story?"

The editor provides a great acid test for you to use when assessing whether you've got a newsworthy story in your business. Ask yourself: Is it enough for the public to care? Is it relevant to the publication? To be honest, answering the first question of who will care could help you answer whether or not it's a newsworthy story. It may sound harsh but it's very important to be cynical and scrutinise your stories. Luckily, there are lots of exercises in this book to help you with this.

A regional news editor said:

"First of all, know the publication you are contacting. It doesn't look great if you only have a vague idea about what we do and who we cater for. I get a number of PRs who ring me up and tell me about a good story and when I ask where it's based, it turns out it's not even in our region!"

That is a big no-no and, again, it's knowing who they write for, knowing the publication, knowing the geographical audience. If you get those things right, you've opened those doors that are initially jammed shut and you've increased your chances of having your story published.

If you don't get those basics right, you could have the most amazing heartwarming story but it doesn't matter. You're wasting your time, you're wasting their time and it means that next time you get in touch, they might be reluctant to see if you've got the right story for them.

That's basically how journalists work. Next, we're going to look at the kind of stories that different journalists look for.

Homework – You probably saw this coming... read some publications that you'd like to be featured in. Do you see any businesses like yours?

What makes the news?

Right, so if I've not overwhelmed you with too much information, we're now going to look at the kind of stories that make the news.

The beauty of this book is that, though there's a lot of detail, you can skim over the sections if you feel they are not relevant to you. However, I would urge you to go through it all once, because then you'll have a solid understanding and be able to marry your business with the relevant stories and publications.

Human interest

I'm going to start with the most heartwarming of all... human interest stories and case studies.

Human interest is what many journalists look for. Unless you're a hard-nosed business journalist who just wants to know about flotations and acquisitions, most journalists look at the human interest angle. They want to know how the story affects me and you. They want to know about what it means for people. Say, for example, you've got a doggy training company and you have a story about a family who just weren't sure how their puppy was going to be trained. Then you came in with your amazing company, trained their dog and now it's like a different canine... it's saved the family time, they've got a better relationship with their pet, and their children have a better relationship with the pet. It's a really heartwarming human interest story.

Here's another example... you've got a homemade organic skin care product aimed at children, which you created because your own child had eczema and allergies and you couldn't find anything on the market for them. It's not so much the product but it's the story and the reasoning *behind* the product that is going to be of interest to a lot of journalists.

I'm going to shamelessly use my own example here. After having generated column inches for clients for over a decade, I decided I wanted some of that sweet publicity for myself when I published my first book, *The Secret Diary of an Arranged Marriage*. In the initial days of its release, I used my backstory to get media coverage.

I had created the first draft of the book in my iPhone notes, writing chapters as I nursed my then one-year-old daughter to sleep. I was pretty sure this was an unusual practice, as most writers would be sitting in front of a computer and, if they're lucky, at their second home at a cliff edge with a sea view (one can dream). Therefore, I leveraged my human interest angle, a mum to a young child penning my debut novel on my phone. It was relatable to a lot of mums who struggle to find time for work around their children. The story received regional coverage and I also starred in a full-page spread in Good Housekeeping magazine about my author journey.

If you're a business-to-business organisation, you might think it's a little harder to find the human interest angle. That might be true to a degree, as you're not aimed at consumers. However, there is a way. Let me give you an example...

Have you ever seen the news when they're talking about the new budgets coming out? It's quite a dry subject, so what you may notice (or I hope you do next time you turn on the news) is that they often say: "Right, now we're going to speak to Keith to see how the new pension budget will affect him..."

Journalists always try to make a business story relatable to people. If there's going to be a new round of investment from the government, or funding is being withdrawn, the journalists will usually get themselves to the floor of a factory to talk to the business owners about how it's going to affect their staff. That's what human interest boils down to - how things affect people.

A while back, when I did the PR for a large healthcare provider, I was always looking for patient case studies to highlight the work of the hospitals.

I secured a full-page spread in the Manchester Evening News, as well as a picture feature on the front cover with a story that had the following headline:

I just want to be able to live my life like any other young woman.

Who wouldn't feel moved by that?

Right off the bat, you know this person doesn't live her life like any other young woman and she wants to.

The background to this story is that a surgeon in one of the hospitals I provided PR for, had a treatment for cerebral palsy. It was a fantastic treatment that helped this girl. It wasn't a cure but it had dramatically improved her quality of life.

When I first interviewed this patient to create the case study, I asked her what kind of things she struggles with.

She replied: "I just want to wear heels. I just want to do normal things. I just want to be a young girl. I'm at university and I want to live my life and I want to be able to go to clubs. I want to be able to do all those things."

That was the heart of the story. She wanted to do what so many others take for granted. I wrote this up as a case study and emailed it to a journalist at the Manchester Evening News, which was one of our key publications as it was read by the hospital's target audience. They were interested in the story because it had such a strong human interest angle. They didn't use the case study word-for-word but they took a lot of key points from there as well as sending a photographer round to take their own pictures of the girl who'd been treated.

Think about your own business - how does it change people's lives? What impact does it have on your community? It doesn't need to be life changing. Even seemingly small improvements make great stories.

If the story was written from the surgeon's perspective, saying how great the procedure is, it wouldn't have had the same impact. In fact, it probably wouldn't have even made the news, as it would just look like an advert. However, by changing the angle to the person benefiting made all the difference.

I pitched another story for my client, an ophthalmic surgeon, about a cataract treatment he performed. Again, the treatment itself isn't that interesting but by writing up a case study of one of his patients, a tennis enthusiast who, pre-surgery, stopped playing for years because her cataracts were getting in the way of her vision, I managed to secure a full-page spread in one of the UK's biggest newspapers, *The Daily Mail*. The story also appeared online and, lucky for my client, even had a link back to their website. Their phone was off the hook with enquiries from that one story.

If you don't have a case study

When I needed to highlight the importance of a healthy diet for our primary healthcare provider client, I pitched to a journalist the idea of inviting a GP to her house to raid her cupboard and assess the 'health' of her kitchen. After appraising her ingredients, the GP showed her how to make a healthy chicken curry.

It was a light-hearted piece with a health message. During the afternoon, the journalist shared that her parents both have diabetes and therefore she was interested in the health implications of her diet. The result was a double-page spread in a regional newspaper.

Making the story about people, as opposed to things, is the gist of a human interest angle. And the media love it.

Homework – Find a human interest angle in your business.

Campaigns

So, we've covered the human interest angle and now I'm going to talk about another area that could work as a story and that is a campaign.

For example, if you've got a yoga studio, a great story could be:

- You want to use yoga to get the elderly fit.
- You want to teach yoga to children because childhood obesity is a growing problem.
- You want to get people outdoors by teaching yoga on a rooftop.

Don't be scared by the word 'campaign'. It doesn't have to mean a huge project with a huge budget and a huge time commitment.

A campaign could simply be a message. When I started my PR consultancy, I was on a bit of a campaign/mission to empower small businesses to do PR because I firmly felt that they shouldn't miss out just because they didn't have deep pockets like a big corporation. As you can tell from reading this book, I'm still on that mission.

I found that a lot of start-ups had a bad experience when they'd done PR because they spent a lot of money on an agency but didn't feel like they got a lot of return. Or the other side was that they hadn't done any PR and they knew it was important. They knew it was crucial for brand awareness, recognition and credibility but they didn't have the budget to do it.

So I did a little survey, which I will cover in more detail in the research section of this book. The main finding was that 71% of start-ups said if they could do their own PR, they would. That was my light bulb moment and the trigger that led to my PR courses and writing this book. It was a story in itself. My campaign was to target start-ups and help fill a gap in the market and that was the story that the journalist had gone with. It featured in a local London paper (as that's where I was living and working at the time and where my target audience resided) with the title: *Entrepreneur sets out to train small firms in how to reach the media.*

I didn't have the campaign you might think of in the traditional sense. It wasn't a big budget. There were no huge banners or posters. I wasn't on a tour bus. The campaign was simply me with a message. I put out a survey and got some intelligence from my target audience (start-ups) and that's how I got my story.

On the other end of the scale, when I worked in healthcare PR, a lot of my clients had campaigns where they wanted to encourage people to eat healthily and make small lifestyle changes that would make a big difference to their health. I pitched our clinical specialist as a spokesperson for the media. We put out case studies, hosted events in town centres and created a lot of buzz in the media.

A campaign could work for you if you're:

- A business coach - you could offer a series of one-to-one sessions for free as your campaign would be to get small business owners thinking like corporate CEOs.

- An author - you could give out eBooks for free as your campaign is to get more people reading.
- A dietitian - you could be urging people to look beyond quick fix diets.
- A fashion brand owner - you could be urging people to avoid fast fashion in favour of timeless, lasting clothing.
- A mum blogger - you could be urging mums to take care of themselves after they give birth.

Another great piece of coverage I secured in City AM (a free London newspaper that everyone reads on the Tube on their way to work) was for a campaign for my client, who was a stress specialist. Her campaign was to make city workers aware that stress is rife in their workplace and to come forward if they need help. That's an example where the campaign was just a really passionate message with a call to action.

Essentially, if you've got something to say and it's strong and relevant, you've potentially got yourself a story that the media will want to hear.

Homework - Come up with two topics you're passionate about that could work for a campaign.

Research

Another kind of story, which is totally doable for any business, is research.

If you've brought out some new research (and it has to be **your** research), you could potentially have a newsworthy story. For example, if you're a freelance HR consultant, you could carry out a survey among HR managers to discover their main pain points when it comes to staff issues. As mentioned in the previous section, research doesn't have to be a huge, expensive undertaking. It could be a survey of 100 or qualitative research among business owners. If the research is interesting enough, or the outcome is interesting enough, you've potentially got yourself a story.

Again, I don't want this book to be theoretical, so, of course, I have a real example for you...

When I worked for an aviation recruitment consultancy, I drafted a press release around some research, which showed that airline HR departments are not as well qualified to assess new pilot candidates as you might think.

Here's a bit of context... being a pilot is no mean feat as they undergo rigorous training and complete hundreds of flight hours to meet the criteria to be able to safely fly you to your holiday. The interesting thing that came out from the research was that not only was there a skills shortage when it came to pilots, but also that airline HR departments were incredibly overworked with hundreds of unsuitable applications to wade through alongside their general HR job. This meant they weren't in the best position to assess the next generation of pilots coming through. This story got a lot of media coverage because it was so pertinent. As a business-to-business (b2b) story, it got into airline publications, HR publications and recruitment publications because it touched on those three different core areas. It goes to show how one good story can gain lots of traction, even across different sector publications.

Think about your business, and not just for the sake of PR, *really* think about what would be interesting for you to find out from your target audience as you may not only stumble across a great story, you might even learn something that helps improve your business model.

Here are some examples:

- If you have a clothing label, you might want to know what's an accessible price point for teenagers.
- If you offer a translation service, you might want to find out what languages are the most requested for translation.
- If you're a children's author, you might want to know how many children in your area have visited their local library.

There are so many different opportunities and the important thing to remember is you are the expert in your field and are therefore best placed to see what kind of research makes the news or what kind of research is interesting to you, because if it's of interest to you, it's quite likely that it might be interesting to your target publications.

How to get PR coverage when it's NOT your

research

While I say it has to be your research, you can also potentially get PR coverage by commenting on big national research or big national stories if you get to a journalist in time. When I was doing PR for a Primary Care Trust, a new research paper came out around parents who smoked in cars and the risks of secondary inhalation for children. Off the back of that research, I quickly got on the phone to the journalist at the Primary Care Trust's local paper. I asked if they'd be interested in an expert comment from my client who's a clinician and could talk in-depth about the research to give them a local angle for the story. The journalist said yes and I secured some great coverage for that client off the back of the national research.

You've probably seen it countless times in the press. Headlines such as:

Local MP condemns government plans.

Local teacher says: schools need more support with funding.

Shop owner supports plans to reduce business rates.

While this approach won't get you on the national news, quite often the local press and radio want a voice from the area to add their opinion to a national topic. That's where you can help.

Homework - Have a think about your areas of expertise. Come up with 3-5 broad topics, which you could comment on if a story were to appear in the media.

Product or service launch

One of the most common news stories is that of a product or service launch.

When you've developed a product, there's usually an audience that would be interested in hearing about it.

It's likely that within your business you'll have such a story at some point, so I wanted to talk about how these stories make the news. Of course, I've got an example for you.

What is a product launch?

A product launch is what it says on the tin. If you're launching a new app, service or physical product, it could be of interest to the media as long as you target correctly.

If you launch an app, there are lots of tech websites that are interested in such stories.

If you're publishing a book, that's technically a new product, too. Your local media and some consumer magazines would want to hear about it.

The story behind the story

Imagine you're launching a range of candles that you've made at home and you ring a journalist and say: "I'm launching this product, can you cover it in your newspaper?"

They'll want to know a bit more about it and ask:

- How do you make these candles?
- Why did you set up this business in your spare time?

Do you see a theme here? Even with a product launch, you can weave in the human interest angle so it's not just a dry *'please promote my product'* plea. You need to give them a story, and sometimes it's the story behind the launch that's of interest.

But wait! I don't have a product. I have a service!

If you're a service provider, you can still get the same kind of coverage but it will be a *service* launch. Same-ish thing, different word. Here's another thing, it doesn't always have to be, dare I say, a brand new service. Sometimes it can be a differentiation in your service.

I secured a big piece of regional coverage with a story about a sign manufacturing client who had partnered with a U.S. company to expand their customer base. However, they'd had an informal affiliation for a while and only recently cemented the partnership. So while it wasn't a new service, the story was that they were partnering with a U.S. company, which added credibility and showed growth and development. They were also a great provider of employment for the city and they had been in business since 1791, adding another localised element to the story.

When thinking of your product or service launch, think what it means to the publication. If it's a niche trade publication specific to your product or service, you can talk about how it's shaping the industry and filling a gap in the market. If it's a local publication, think of the impact on the community. Are you creating new jobs? Are you bringing something new to the area? Are you a local business done good? Make it relevant to the journalist, paper, or website you're targeting.

When I pitched the sign manufacturing partnership story to the manufacturing trade press, I used a different angle. They didn't want to know that it was a Nottingham-based company that had been in operation since 1791 and were creating jobs in the area. They wanted to know about the partnership and what it means for the business.

Different journalists and different publications require different approaches but the beauty is that the same story can have multiple bites of the cherry, getting you even more news coverage.

Homework - Have you launched a product or service that would be of interest to the media? Note it down.

Business development

Another sure-fire way of getting yourself column inches with credibility is if you have a business development or a notable hire. This doesn't have to be a big recruitment drive or acquisition. If you're a team of three and you've appointed another person, that's still growth and would be deemed newsworthy.

A business development angle might be that you're going into a new market or targeting a new demographic.

As always, context is everything, and I have some examples for you.

When my private healthcare client was appointed as executive director of three hospitals, I knew it had all the trappings of a great news story. Yes, it was a business development story and a notable hire but my client was from the area within which she would be working and was a mum of three. It was a great example of a local woman's success. The human interest angle played into the story, which I pitched to the regional press, resulting in a half-page spread in the paper.

When I pitched a similar new hire to the business press, I stuck to the professional credentials of the director. As hard-nosed as it sounds, the journalist wasn't interested in the family background of the appointee. They wanted to know about their previous role, years of experience, etc. They published the story and went with the straightforward title: "Healthcare firm appoints a new executive director."

With the two examples, you can see that different types of publications require different angles for the same business development story, just as they do for product launches, as I mentioned in the previous section.

It might seem bewildering but there's actually a quite straightforward formula when it comes to writing and pitching these stories and rest assured, I'm going to walk you through, step-by-step, so you know exactly how to recreate this formula for your business.

Why should I be in a business publication? I'm a consumer business!

If you're in the business-to-consumer sector, you may be thinking: "Why would I want to get into a business publication? They're not my target audience!"

I would say that while it might not be your top priority, any kind of positive PR helps because it shows your credibility. If you're a start-up and you're looking for your first, second or third round of investment, your potential investors will be interested to hear that you've got media coverage around your brand's development. It shows that you mean business. It shows that you're here to stay and you're invested. It's also a great opportunity to get yourself across different publications and in front of new audiences. And if I've not said this before, I'll say it now... getting great PR levels you up with the competition, including the big competitors with big PR budgets. It shows that you must be good at what you do, as you've got the media coverage to prove it.

Homework - Note down any business developments you have that may be of interest to the media.

Awards

Even though looking through a newspaper may leave you thinking that there's a bad-news-is-good-news agenda, journalists love to praise small businesses that have done well and an award win is a great example of this.

If you own a restaurant and you've entered yourself into a relevant award and you win (or you're even nominated) that's a great story. You need to make sure that you're shouting about these things and picking up the phone to journalists to tell them you have won an award or been highly commended. They would love to hear about it. It's not just a local story. If it's a national award (i.e. a national curry award) you can go to food trade publications and share the story with them, too.

Not only will an awards-based story give you credibility, the media will always champion a business done good.

Almost every industry has relevant awards to enter. If you write a blog, you could enter a blogger award within your niche. If you're an author, there are numerous awards - big and small - for different genres. I entered my debut book, *The Secret Diary of an Arranged Marriage*, into two awards. It won the public vote for the Page Turner Awards and won the BookBrunch Selfie Award for Best Adult Fiction. I wrote press releases off the back of both award wins, which resulted in media coverage, publicity and a boost in sales of my book.

If you've not entered any awards before, think about getting yourself out there because not only does the award give you a huge amount of kudos, the PR off the back of it gives you the kind of boost that money cannot buy. What more reason is there to get your award submissions in?

Homework - Look into the awards in your sector. Are there any you'd be eligible to enter?

Thought leadership

Another great way of generating fantastic PR that positions you as an expert in your field and makes you the go-to authority in your sector is advice articles and commentary pieces, or as we PR folk like to call it - thought leadership.

Advice and tips pieces are so relevant, particularly in this online world, because there are many publications for all the different sectors out there, needing to hear from experts like you.

One prominent sector is the small business sector and there are an abundance of publications catering for this. Just some examples are businessadvice.co.uk and Real Business. While publications like these have lots of news stories, they also feature advice and guides because their readers are going on there, looking for tips and resources to help their business grow and thrive.

As you're an expert in your field, think about the advice you can offer.

For example, if you're an executive coach, what are the tips to help people reduce stress in the workplace? What do you need to include in the perfect business plan? What are the publications that you've read that offer those kinds of tips?

Once you have your answers, you could get in touch with the relevant publications to offer your expertise, whether that's in the form of an article or your top five tips.

The benefits of advice and guides are manifold:

- Journalists welcome them. If you're offering quality

content to them for free, they'd be inclined to use it.

- The person reading the publication (your target audience) will think: *This person definitely knows their stuff.*
- The content is usually evergreen and not time-sensitive.
- They are handy to have when you don't have any product or service launches or human interest stories.

There is also space for advice pieces in the general / mainstream press, though this would usually be in the form of a press release with a call-to-action, rather than top tips.

I secured an article in City AM for my stress specialist client, with the headline: *Businesses are urged to address the issue of stressed out city workers.* It wasn't a news story, but it was a strong opinion-led piece that was very pertinent to the publication. For context, there's quite a macho culture in the City of London, where it's commonly perceived that stress doesn't happen. If it does, it's a sign of weakness. My client wanted to dispel that myth and say employers need to realise it's more common than they think and is affecting their revenue and their bottom line in ways they don't realise. Presenteeism is a huge issue, with people turning up to work tired and stressed but they'll never admit to it because of the culture. As a result, their productivity drops. My client's call to action was totally relevant to that publication and is a great example of how a strong piece of advice can make the news.

Here are some examples for different sectors:

- If you have a beauty product, your advice could be

around using sunscreen all year around.

- If you've created a tech product, you can talk about the need to innovate in your sector.
- If you're a business coach, you can talk about the importance of maintaining a work/life balance whilst working from home.
- If you're a life coach, you could talk about visualisation and manifestation.
- If you're an author, you may have an opinion around your story (i.e. if you write historical fiction, you can talk about your research around the era). For my book *The Secret Diary of an Arranged Marriage*, I pitched thought leadership pieces on the misconceptions of the topic. I was featured on BBC radio as well as national and regional publications.

Homework - Think of three topics you can share your expertise on and position yourself as a thought leader.

The right stories for the right media

I've talked about what makes the news and now I want to break it down further and detail the different kinds of stories and criteria that are set by the various publication types.

For example, in your business you might have a story that is perfect for a national publication, or you might have a story that lends itself to an online news site, or you might have a great local story.

The entire purpose of this section is to help you target the different media outlets appropriately, because you might find that some stories in your business work for a few different mediums, and they'll each require different approaches.

This section breaks down what the different journalists look for so you can ensure that when you're pitching your story, you're pitching it right. Starting with national stories.

National stories

When I talk about national media, I'm referring to the national press and national broadcast media.

Here's a fact - getting national media coverage is hard, but not impossible.

Below are some criteria:

First to market

The national press want the groundbreaking things like a national or international first.

While there are other things that can make a national news story, being the first to market is a sure-fire way. If you have a product, it really has to be up there and add real value. For example, if you're developing an app, you have to ask yourself whether it offers something that is a complete game changer in your industry.

The thing to remember is when you go national with a story, unless it's a feature, you are competing with stories across the nation, and therefore it has to be of relevance to readers and viewers from all over the country.

Think about your product or service. Is it groundbreaking? Does it fulfil the criteria mentioned above?

Human interest

I've touched upon this before. Human interest angles are absolutely key for national media. Stories need to be relatable and case studies help with this.

If you've launched a new product, do you have an ideal customer that has been through the process of using your product? How was it for them? That's where a story really comes to life.

Often, when I'm pitching a national story, the journalist would come back and say: "That sounds great. Have you got a case study to go with it?" They want to illustrate the story through an individual and bring it down to the human interest angle. So whilst I would get in touch saying that my client has got this fantastic product, the journalist would be interested in hearing it from someone else to further verify the benefits I was talking about. That's where a human interest case study comes in.

Themes that tap into a national debate

Think about what's going on in your country. Think about what is the general feel in society. Here in the UK, we've had Brexit, many political shakeups and that pandemic that changed the world.

Speaking of Covid, an ongoing story has been the fallout for small businesses and whether the government has done enough to support them. Business owners up and down the country, from pub landlords to boutique owners to start-ups, were featured in the national news to talk about how they were managing during the crisis. There were stories about people pivoting with their businesses. The point is, when there is a subject of national interest, journalists often look for businesses/people who can share what it's like 'in the trenches'.

A national issue that everybody's talking about

Think about where you can add to the conversation with your product or service. What need is it catering for? Does it tap into a national debate or can you add value by saying something different to the national debate?

When it comes to a big story, journalists are looking for somebody who's going to be able to voice or have an expert opinion on the issue.

For example, if you're an accountant, you could provide an expert comment when the budgets come out or when there are new tax regulation rules.

Here's the thing, being the first to market is rare, as is having a national first. However, tapping into a national debate with an expert comment is a relatively easy (or certainly more accessible) way of getting national media coverage for your business.

A little (more) etiquette

When pitching to a national journalist, expect them to follow up, want interviews and take their own pictures.

One of the things I've noticed in my time as a PR consultant and as a former journalist is that the local or even regional media are often happy to take your content as it is. If you provide a print-ready press release for them, they're quite happy to use that, often verbatim. They'll usually use the picture you send, too.

However, I've never had a situation where a national journalist has covered one of my stories word-for-word off the back of my press release, no matter how beautifully its been crafted. As a general rule, national journalists tend to follow up, do their own checks and balances and get exclusive content, interviews and angles to make sure that their story is unique to their publication. They'll want to take their own pictures that they'll own the rights to. Essentially, they're very thorough in making sure that they have the story from their angle.

Also, as an aside, it's worth noting that a lot of the national journalists are freelancers, so they're expected to write it all up and do their homework and not just use a press release.

Therefore bear in mind that if you send over a press release and they're interested and they want to follow up, they may well ask for an interview and they may want to arrange a time to take pictures, whether it's of yourself and your product, or a case study you've put forward.

Pitch perfect

I mentioned this previously when I talked about how journalists operate, they're very short on time. They do not have the hours in the day to indulge someone talking war and peace about their story. You need to pitch concisely. The top information has to be front and centre so it's easy for them to decide if it's a story that's of relevance.

A good way of thinking about it is that if a local journalist has a flooded inbox, a national journalist has a tsunami of press releases sent to them every day. You're competing for them to open your mail with all those other press releases and pitches that have been sent to them, so you need to make sure that your story is tight and concise and the top line is enough for them to say: "Right, I want to find out more about this story."

Being geographically appropriate

This might go without saying but it's worth a mention. National journalists will be most interested in the stories from their country. If you're in the US, they're mainly interested in US issues. Australian publications will focus on Australian issues, etc. However, national journalists will invite comment or features on international issues.

Open any of your national newspapers. There will be stories about the country primarily. However, they do have space for world news and features. It's just something to bear in mind and be aware that your story potentially has legs outside of your own country if you can position it right.

Personalisation

Don't take a one-size-fits-all approach. This is important for all publications but no more so than national titles. National newspapers have different leanings, different political views, different audiences and different styles of writing. You can see this by simply opening up a newspaper.

The Times features articles written with a lot of detail, whereas the Daily Mail is more consumer-leaning as a newspaper. It has more pictures, shorter articles.

With that in mind, it really won't do to send one blanket press release to all the publications, unless of course you've got something like an international first and they'll be scrambling for your story. You have to adopt a tailored approach, creating a specific pitch relevant to the publication.

If you take the above points into consideration when pitching your story to the national press, it greatly increases your chances of getting quality coverage.

It's a lot to take in, right? Rest assured, we're going to look at examples of national stories I've worked on. Hopefully, that will give you some real context in terms of where all these points fit in.

National examples

I want to share with you some examples of what national stories look like.

These are all real examples that have appeared in the national media, so they should help give you an even better idea of the kind of stories that would make the cut.

Here's one point though - newspapers and magazines have strict rules about sharing their content. You cannot use screenshots or scans of their articles, which is why I can't include any in this book. Instead, you're going to have to do a spot of visualising. But if you've ever read a newspaper or magazine (which I'm sure you have), you'll have no trouble picturing the coverage I'm talking about.

Headline: Music brings harmony to dementia patients

This piece appeared in the Guardian newspaper in the UK. It was about half a page of coverage with pictures.

The story was a case study about a care home where the residents, who have dementia, took part in interactive music sessions, which were designed to help them reminisce, encourage conversation, evoke memories and build communication. Dementia residents often struggle with communication and memory, which affects their interaction with loved ones as well as carers at the home.

You don't need to read in a lot of detail to realise that this story has a strong human interest angle.

Dementia is such a heartbreaking condition and it's something that is very much at the forefront of people's minds in the UK. Many people know somebody who's been touched by dementia, so it was very relevant. At the time of publication, dementia was all over the news because there was a new care bill and much discussion around what to do with our ageing population, so it really struck the right note.

The other reason this story was so compelling was because the journalist was invited to come and see a session for themselves and then have conversations with the carers at the home, as well the residents and their loved ones. The interactive element of getting the journalist involved in the case study and the fact that it was such a moving issue *and* there were people to illustrate the story is what really helped bring this piece to life and make it worthy of its place in a national publication.

Headline: Tiny sling correcting uterine prolapse spares women trauma of hysterectomy

This is a story that appeared in the Daily Mail newspaper and the Mail online. It's a case study I wrote up of a patient who was treated for uterine prolapse with a procedure that spares women the trauma of a hysterectomy, which previously was the alternative option.

The article was a full-page with a photo of the woman who received the treatment, which was taken by one of the newspaper's photographers.

You can hopefully see a theme here. There's a strong human interest angle. The woman who had the treatment was interviewed and pictured in the newspaper, looking happy and smiling having had this life changing treatment.

It's her story and focuses on the reason she needed to have the procedure. She shares how her life was living with the condition, versus how it is now. It's a case study of someone illustrating the story rather than the surgeon just explaining the procedure. Without the patient's perspective, it would have been quite a dry medical story, but instead it was a human interest and lifestyle story that got national coverage.

The other factor which helped secure the coverage was that as it was a gynaecological condition, it wasn't talked about, yet many women suffered from it. It's something that was seen as embarrassing and that women wouldn't want to discuss, so putting it out there sent a message that those suffering with this weren't alone.

Headline: Five must read business books for ambitious entrepreneurs

This story wasn't breaking news but instead more of a feature-based story and the kind of thing where you can add comment. This was in an offshoot of the Telegraph, called Telegraph Connect, which is a part of the newspaper aimed at small businesses. It was a paragraph of coverage without a picture.

The journalist reached out via Twitter for book recommendations from business owners and entrepreneurs, and I responded to them with my recommendation (if you're interested, I recommended The Miracle Morning by Hal Elrod). As a result, I secured coverage for my PR consultancy. It was only a small mention, but my business was name checked in the publication, which helped with my SEO and added credibility to my business, having been featured in a national paper as an expert.

I mentioned previously, if you haven't got a groundbreaking story or a great human interest case study, it's not to say the national media will be elusive to you as there are opportunities like the above example.

If you can build a dialogue with a national journalist (and I'm going to show you how later on in this book), then this kind of opportunity would be ideal for your business, as it's a quick and easy way to secure national coverage.

There are many ways of getting coverage through commenting. Here are a few examples:

- If there's a national political story and you've got something to add from your business perspective.
- If there's a financial story and you're an accountant, lawyer or a financial advisor with something to say on the subject.
- If there's a story about education and you have a parenting blog or related business, which is affected by the story.
- If you have a shop or cafe, you can comment on the business rates.

These are just some opportunities you could piggyback on to get national coverage of your own.

Headline: 'It's been one of the most rewarding experiences of my life'

Did I mention I wrote a book?

I reached out to Good Housekeeping, who were looking for women who'd made big life changes over lockdown. I pitched my story... how I'd fulfilled a lifelong ambition by writing and publishing a novel. In my pitch I mentioned how I'd first wrote a 60,000-word children's book at the age of 12, sent it to Penguin amongst other publishers and was rejected by them all. I shared how I wrote the first draft of my debut book, *The Secret Diary of an Arranged Marriage*, on my iPhone notes, hired my own editor and cover designer.

I detailed the response to the book, having won awards and read an excerpt on a Facebook live with a 100k+ strong group that was my target audience, and how the success spurred me on to write a follow up to the story.

The pitch was strong enough for Good Housekeeping to interview me, send over a photographer and hair and makeup and dedicate a full-page spread to my story.

Best of all, they not only plugged my book, which resulted in sales, they mentioned that the second book, *The Secret Diary of a Bengali Bridezilla* was due out, too.

Headline: Can't care won't care: third of Brits would not look after elderly parents

This was actually a story that came off the back of a survey that was carried out amongst the general public. It was a large spread of coverage with a stock photo of a pensive looking older woman.

As the title suggests, the key point was that a third of adults wouldn't look after their parents when the time came that they needed full-time support.

This story made waves at the time and generated a huge amount of media coverage. I think there was a sense of surprise that people wouldn't look after their parents in their old age.

This story did two things:

- It featured research with a sizeable population sample. If you do a survey and you're aiming at the national press, it really has to have legs - you need at least a thousand respondents because anything smaller is seen as not representative enough of the general population.
- It hit at the right time when people were talking about elderly parents, the ageing population and dementia. It was a topic frequently featured in the news.

I hope the examples above bring to life what makes the national news and crucially, show you what is achievable for your business.

Homework – can you think of any stories within your business that may interest the national media?

Right stories - Regional

The regional and local media will be a source of great PR opportunities for you, because local and regional publications love championing businesses from their area.

Here's how to get their interest...

It seems like a no-brainer but I really can't emphasise this enough - the story needs to be relevant to the area. Whether you're in Manchester, England, or Manchester, New Hampshire, your story needs to relate to the Manchester which the publication serves.

When I shared the things that irked journalists earlier on in this book, pitching a geographically inappropriate story was top of the list.

Believe it or not, many people send stories that aren't relevant for the area or the journalist. This usually happens when they send a blanket press release and they blind copy the world into it, sending it to every journalist under the sun. All too often it goes into the wrong inbox, resulting in the already inundated journalist receiving yet another irrelevant story. That's why it's even more important to make sure that you're targeting the right journalist for your story.

Another tip (and I will go into detail on this later on) is if you've got a story that is interesting both nationally and regionally, they do require a different approach. For example, when writing a press release for a regional journalist, you'll want to emphasise in the subject line of the email that it's a story local to that region. For example, the title could be *Manchester business does xxx* (whatever the story is). However, you wouldn't need to put the location front and centre for a national story, as it would be of interest to the whole of the UK.

Keep it relevant

A mistake people often make is submitting a story with a tenuous link to the region. As an example, if you've got a business that sells jewellery and you're based in Manchester, New Hampshire, it's totally fine to go to the local press there because you're from that area. However, if you sell online and have customers in various places across the country, that in itself is not enough to get in publications in the different areas that you sell jewellery, because it's just too tenuous.

It won't do to say: "Okay, my business is based in London but I send products to Scotland and Ireland and have suppliers in Birmingham, so journalists in those areas would be interested in my stories."

Sadly, that's not enough to make it relevant to those regions. You've got to have a strong link, i.e. your business is based there, or you've got a customer that's happy to be a case study and the story is all about them and they are based in that region.

Regionals like print-ready stories

A big difference between regional and national publications is that nationals try to get more information and write original copy. The journalist will conduct their own interviews and often they'll want to take their own photos. Whereas with regionals and certainly the local press, they prefer their stories print-ready. They don't have the same capacity as national journalists, nor do they work in the same way. They also follow a different news agenda. Therefore, as long as you are local to the publication and the story is relevant, your chances of having your story published are high. That's not to say they'll always use your press release word-for-word. However, in my experience, if the copy is crafted the way they'd like to write it and you've included all the essential information (more on this later), the chances of them printing it almost exactly as you sent it is quite high because the journalist is less likely to come digging for information.

Of course, there are exceptions to the rule. There have been occasions where I've pitched stories and the regional or local journalist has wanted an interview or more information but, generally speaking, they want things print-ready and would prefer a full press release over a few bullet points. It makes their job easier and you've got more chance of getting their attention.

Regionals love a good photo

When it comes to local and regional print and online media, it's always better to have a good picture to go with the story. More often than not, they'll happily use the photo you send, as opposed to sending their photographer to take their own pictures. Again, I'll use the caveat that there are exceptions to the rule. Occasionally, I've sent press releases with photos and the journalist has said: "That's great, can we send our photographer to get a picture of the business owner, or take a picture of the case study?" However, it makes their life easier if you've got a great picture that you can send along with your print-ready press release. And if you can make their life easier, you greatly increase your chances of getting some nice PR coverage.

Send small files

All journalists, whether they're national, regional or local, have limited email inbox capacities, so if you email over a picture that's more than 1mb, they might not love you for it because you'll probably destroy their inbox. When sending something to a journalist, get a good picture but keep it small. If they require a higher resolution image, they will ask you for it.

A note about broadcast media

For regional broadcast media (i.e. local TV and radio) it is different because they're going to need their own video or audio footage so they are likely to come and conduct interviews with you. However, the same rules apply - make sure your story is relevant to that area, make your pitch print-ready and don't flood their inbox with huge pictures.

Regional examples

Now we're going to look at some real examples of regional articles to help you discover the kind of stories that you may have right under your nose that would be of interest to the regional and local media.

Headline: Special guest casts her eye around medical marvel

This story was about the launch of a new CT scanner at a local hospital. It might sound like a dry subject but it was brought to life with a really nice picture where we'd got the director of the hospital and the local mayor, who we'd invited along to the launch, peering through the scanner and smiling. The paper didn't use much of the press release. Instead, they lead with a big version of the picture and had three short columns of text underneath.

As it was an investment in the hospital that would help patients in the community, it ticked all the boxes for a great regional story, hence securing a quarter-page spread in the newspaper.

Headline: Stockport mum penned award-winning novel on phone notes app while raising two kids

This article appeared in the Manchester Evening News and its online version. It was about my award win for *The Secret Diary of an Arranged Marriage*.

With all due bias, this story was the perfect recipe for the media. It featured an award win, a human-interest, against-the-odds angle and a local person done good.

The fact that I wrote the first draft of my book on my iPhone notes while my daughter slept (on me) made it aspirational. That I'd entered the awards and then forgot about it until I was shortlisted, added a quirky element.

I also sent a photo to go with the story, where I'm casually leaning against a bookshelf. Having a print-ready photo made the journalist's job all that easier.

I reached out with a press release but the journalist called me for an interview, which is where he found out more about my unusual writing method (no seafront office for me. I utilise my phone for initial drafting even today). He used that for his headline.

Headline: Julie drops in to open kids' clinic at hospital

For context, Julie is well known in Manchester as she is a footballer's wife and she also has her own health food business. She was invited to the launch of a new paediatric unit at a private hospital, where her daughter had been treated when she was younger. Julie had a real connection with the hospital and was very keen to be involved in the opening. The great thing about this launch was that we did it on a very small budget. As it was a children's unit we decided on having a Christmas launch for the media with a Santa's grotto for the children who were staying at the hospital.

The children (whose parents had already consented to have their pictures in the media) visited the grotto, sat on Santa's knee, got a present and just had a really nice time.

We got two columns of coverage alongside a nice picture of Julie, Santa, and a child at the grotto. This story was also featured in numerous other publications.

The media love these heartwarming stories, especially if they allow for cute pictures of young children (tip: the media love animals, too. The saying *never work with children or animals* doesn't apply to the press).

This story also played into some important factors:

- There was a human interest angle.
- It was relevant to the area.
- There was a celebrity / familiar face for the story and photo opps.
- I provided print-ready copy for the journalist who attended the launch. They mostly lifted the copy from my press release, which reinforces my previous point. If it's easier for the journalist, they're more likely to cover your story.

Also, it helped that I arranged a small spread of cakes and snacks for the journalists attending the launch. Many of the photographers and press who attended hung back to have some snacks. So, if in doubt, throw cake into the mix.

The great news for you is that beyond buying a few presents and getting some decorations, it wasn't a huge investment (in time or money) but it gave a great PR return.

Headline: US link a sign of the times for firm founded in 1791

Quite a different story here, as it's an example of some regional business PR coverage. The story is about the partnership between a US and UK company. The UK company in question (my client) is a sign manufacturer based in Nottingham. They are a well established company that was founded in 1791, so there's a lot of heritage and history embedded in the community. Even though it's a business story, you can see that by bringing in some context around how old the company is, you get a localised story.

The journalist not only covered the story but they did an interview because they wanted some more information and they also sent around a photographer to take pictures.

It was PR magic for us because they'd invested time to make the story right for them, which resulted in almost a whole page of coverage.

Headline: Businesses must focus on a vision

The story was about my client, an executive coach, giving the call-to-action to local businesses saying that to become a bigger player and grow their business they need to act like a bigger business, think long term and create a vision for the future.

It was a great business story because it was asking people to make a change. It was urging businesses to do *something*. It's an advice piece but because it's focused on the area from which the client comes from, it was relevant. If it was a story about a client based in London urging businesses in Manchester to do something, it wouldn't really be relevant because it's too tenuous and there isn't a local connection.

Because my executive coach client was from that locality and she was urging local businesses in her area to do something, it was a stronger story.

Headline: Leyton man sets up new search engine to support world sanitation projects

As you can tell from the title, it was a new product launch and was featured in one of the local papers within the Guardian group. You can also see that they used his location, Leyton, in the title to add local relevance.

The title is a bit of a mouthful, but the article includes lots of information (mostly taken from my press release) to explain the story in more detail. Essentially, he's a local guy doing great things. Not only was he launching a new search engine but it was going to help sanitation projects around the world. The local media jumped on it. While the story started with the Guardian, the TV station London Live, upon seeing the coverage, interviewed my client. This goes to show that sometimes you can get a lot of mileage out of your stories, because journalists often look at other publications to see what stories are making the news. A positive news story can run and run.

Headline: Wonder diet that's helping us win battle with diabetes

This case study, which I pitched for my healthcare client, appeared in a Scottish regional publication. It was about a couple that had been diagnosed with diabetes (disclaimer: don't try this at home before speaking to your doctor) and were advised by their dietitian to go on a specific liquid diet, which helped them manage their diabetes.

This was a relevant story because it had a human interest angle, it was health related and it was a pertinent topic. Of course, the couple were from the area in Scotland that the paper covers.

Headline: Wellbeing charity gets £2,000 boost for funds

This is a nice heartwarming local story about a charity that received £2,000 for being a runner-up in a competition.

There's a bit in the copy about the charity itself and what they do and why it was set up but the headline itself was self-explanatory. This had the perfect mix of:

- A local charity
- An award / prize win
- A feel-good story about something positive in the community

Headline: Patients score hospital 98.8%

Last, but not least, here's an example of a survey-based story. It's about a hospital that scored 98.8% for service in its patient satisfaction survey. This was an internal survey conducted amongst patients at the hospital on how they felt about their treatment and stay. The number of respondents was very small as it was conducted when patients were discharged (if you've ever stayed in hospital you may have seen a similar thing, it's usually a small sheet with some boxes to tick).

The hospital did quite well from it, so I went with the headline that hospitals had received the ultimate accolade from the people that matter the most.

This goes to show that for local and regional media, you don't have to have a huge sample of respondents for it to be of relevance. Even a smaller number of 100, or less if it's qualitative research, can still get you column inches.

If you do a customer / client satisfaction survey and the results are positive, that might well be a story that can get you into the local or regional media.

Homework - From the examples above, have a think about what stories you have that may fit the criteria for a local or a regional story. Consider any partnerships, affiliations, new business developments, or awards that will work for your local and regional media.

Right stories – Trade

So we've covered the right stories for the right media when it comes to the national, local and regional media. Now I wanted to focus on the trade press.

Trade media explained

Sorry if this feels like teaching you to suck eggs, however I thought it's worth clarifying what trade media is.

Trade media is business-to-business media that is industry specific. They're not aimed at the public. They're aimed at people that read these publications to get an understanding of the industry.

The majority of businesses I work with have trade media targets, even if they've got some consumer-facing services or products.

For example, if you're a law firm, you might have trade publications that you want to get into. If you're an accountancy firm or a business services firm and your key clients are other businesses, you might want to get into business specific publications.

If you're a business coach or stress specialist and you work with HR departments, you might want to target the HR press. If you're an author of non-fiction, you might want to target publications within the speciality you write about. If you're a fiction author, you may write in specialist publications if your books have a particular niche, i.e. military, RAF.

A note - trade isn't just restricted to the print press anymore. There are lots of online publications aimed at specific industries. However, I'm focusing on print trade magazines here, because I am going to cover online media as a separate part of the book.

I've already given you a few examples of the kind of publications that could work for your industry. Now, I want to detail what they look for in a story.

You can be as technical as you like

No matter what industry you're in or what trade publication you target, one thing that separates them from the local, regional and national consumer press is that trade publication articles can be very technical.

If you recall, when I talked about the stories that work for the local and regional media, one of the examples I shared was of a new CT scanner. The angle I went with was that we'd invited the local mayor and we took a really nice picture of her with the executive director peering through the scanner. We led with the fact that it would help people who have suffered with claustrophobia and who struggled to be in tight spaces because it's a wider scanner. That's about as technical as we got and the focus was on us inviting the mayor and how it was a great boost for the hospital and local community.

The same CT scanner story was pitched to the trade media but the angle we went with was nothing to do with the mayor. The trade press wouldn't be interested. They wanted to know that it's a new scanner and what it does. For example, one of the trade titles that we targeted was RAD magazine, which is all about radiology.

They wanted to know the spec of the scanner, what type of scanner it was and what the benefits were. The fact that it was wider, so it helped with claustrophobic as well as overweight patients, was of interest. They really wanted to get down to the nitty-gritty, technical aspect of the scanner.

Think about what kind of stories you might have in your business. If you've got a product or service launch, would it be relevant to trade publications? Do you know the trade publications in your sector?

Quite often, I go into small law and accountancy firms and they have the standard publications on their coffee table. What are the standard publications in your industry? What are people reading? Have a look and think about where you could fit in.

One thing I can guarantee is if you look at the trade publications, you will find that they are a lot more technical because they are aimed at an already educated audience. It's assumed that the audience of a trade magazine will have a certain level of knowledge about what you're talking about. RAD magazine already knew what a scanner was. They didn't need it spelt out for them. They needed to find out what type of scanner it was and what it would do.

Local and non-national stories could work

Using the example of the scanner, it was a local story but it also worked as a trade story. It wouldn't work for the national press - we couldn't make any big claims like the scanner was groundbreaking, or the best of its kind. However, trade publications by and large are often national, if not international. They don't have geographical boundaries like local and regional stories. They are defined by their sector, rather than their location. So while your local story might not have legs for a national consumer publication, it could get into trade media and reach far and wide to your target audience.

One of my former clients was a small aviation recruitment firm, and I managed to get them into several aviation specific publications. This added a huge amount of gravitas to their business and helped them stand out amongst their peers. While trade might have smaller circulation numbers than a national and even some local publications, it's targeted PR. People read these publications because they want the industry news. They're a more interested audience than someone who reads a national newspaper that covers a range of topics.

How trade could work for you

If your business is selling eco-friendly, vegan, allergen-free baby products, you'd likely want to get yourself into the consumer media because you want mums to read about it.

If you wanted to look at trade angles, you could think about what's new about the product. Whether it's made in an innovative way. Whether there are unusual ingredients. Then you'd look at what publications would be interested in these angles. For example, you'd look at vegan-focussed magazines, or retail publications aimed at buyers. Put simply, looking at trade allows you to explore other ways to get to your stakeholders beyond the consumer media.

It's always worth thinking when you've got a local story, whether there's a trade angle that would give you two bites of the cherry.

You'd have to tweak it slightly differently, which is what we're going to talk about later, but essentially, your story could go beyond just being a local story and it could reach nationally without getting into the big national papers.

Keep it relevant

As mentioned, it has to be relevant to the specialty. If you're targeting Plastics and Rubber Weekly (to the uninitiated, yes, that's a real publication), which is very technical, you have to have something of relevance to them.

With my aviation client, the publications were only interested in aviation-based stories and even within those publications sometimes it's a particular area of aviation. It might be Aviation Security, which is a publication in itself, or it might be Airline Business, which is all about the business of aviation, or it might be a more technical aerospace publication. The point is, take care and attention when targeting.

Get a copy of the publication, read over a few stories and familiarise yourself. See whether you can add something to that publication or tailor your story to them.

Exclusivity helps

Sometimes, trade publications prefer an exclusive angle. This is because trade publications are few and far between and they don't often go for the blanket catch-all press releases you could send to your consumer media.

They would need it tweaked to fit their editorial. This isn't to say that you have to constantly rewrite your press releases to fit the various trade titles, but sometimes tweaking an angle, tweaking the top line, making an element of it exclusive to them gives you more advantages.

I gave you the example of my aviation client previously. I got them in Airline Business by offering an exclusive opinion piece from one of the directors.

Another example from the same client in aviation is that we did a story that was all about the business of running airlines from an airport's perspective. We then pitched the story from the pilot's perspective to a very specific publication called Pilot Career News.

Often, just getting in touch with the journalist and offering the top line to them and explaining why the story is relevant, what exclusive angle and exclusive quote you can offer is enough to pique their interest. The beauty of this is that you can gauge their interest before writing a whole article for them.

Longer articles work well

With the trade press, longer articles work well because you can afford to be technical to make it more relevant.

For national, regional and local media, press releases shouldn't go beyond one page. However, the trade press are often interested in longer angles and this goes back to the exclusivity angle. For example, when I've worked in the architectural and buildings press, I've looked at their respective trade publications and pitched specific articles depending on their content. One magazine had a section on eco-friendly buildings and when I pitched a relevant angle, they came back with a request for me to write a 500-800 word article.

This, of course, is way beyond the traditional press release, but the trade magazines have the capacity for it. If you do pitch and a publication requests a 500 or 800 word article, don't be daunted. You should be ecstatic, because the more words they want, the more space they will give to your business in their magazine, and the greater the chance of your brand getting out there and really resonating with your target audience.

A note about colour separation

This might not be relevant to you depending on your industry but I just wanted to cover all bases, because as I've mentioned previously, this book is aimed at *any* small business in any industry.

If you don't know, a colour separation is like an advert. It's a paid for piece that comes off the back of a press release. Some trade publications only take paid for articles, so it's something to bear in mind if your target publications have colour separations.

When I started out in PR, I didn't know what colour separations were. I was trained on the notion that if your story is good enough, it will get coverage for free. After all, that's what separates PR from advertising, right?

However, certain industry magazines (and this is particularly prevalent in property and construction, buildings and architectural trade press) can't afford to print stories for free. Their only way of survival is through charging PR companies and businesses for their articles. Often, after pitching a story, they'll come back to you and say: "We love the story. We've got a quarter-page of space and we can do you a deal. It's £100/$100 to have a 300-word article in our magazine." To all intents and purposes, it's an advert, or at least an advertorial.

If you pitch a story to a trade magazine and are met with a colour separation offer, do not think that your story isn't good enough to be printed for free. If you've got a small budget, this may be an option. If not, there are still plenty of trade publications that will print your story free of charge. As you get more familiar with the various trade magazines out there, you'll see which titles take colour separations and which ones will print your article without a fee.

Trade press have more forward features

A forward feature is essentially a feature opportunity happening in the future, which you could potentially be a part of.

A lot of journalists work to a yearly schedule. For example, Vogue has a September edition that everybody wants to be in and that's the one that they really work towards.

Trade publications often have a calendar of forward feature opportunities. The architectural press might cover eco buildings for October, and then they might be covering buildings on a budget in November, whereas December might be all about the more high-end and high-spec buildings.

As another example, a lot of the retail trade magazines start planning for Christmas features in July.

Finding the forward feature opportunities is simple. It's a case of picking up the phone and asking them if they have a list of the forward features they'll be working on over the next six months or year. They'll probably be happy to send it to you, enabling you to see what opportunities they have and put your hat in the ring to contribute to their features. You'd pitch by saying: "I've noticed in April you're doing something about affordable homes. I am a builder and I work on affordable homes so could I put an article forward on *xyz* (whatever your exclusive angle is)?" If your angle works for them, then you've secured yourself a great piece of trade media coverage.

Trade examples

Here are some examples of what trade stories look like:

Headline: Business launches new product to boost security and efficiency at smaller airports

This was for one of my old clients that produced ID pass applications and it appeared in a publication called Aviation Securities International. It was about the launch of a new product that was going to be helpful for smaller airports that are often underserved and overlooked in favour of the biggest airports in the world.

Had I pitched the story locally, I would have focused on the fact that it's a business from that area. I would have detailed what it's planning to do and its ambitions for growth. However, as this was an international trade publication, they didn't need to know about it being a local business done good. They wanted to hear about what this product did, what was different about it and who would benefit from it. It was those points that made it an interesting story. To put this piece together, I had to interview my client with my journalist hat on to really understand what is new and different, who it's going to help, and, crucially, how it would change the industry.

I've talked about the key questions that you need to look at and the key questions that journalists ask. As you progress through this book, we are going to dig deeper to find the best stories in your business. For now, I'm really hoping this story gives you an example of what kind of angle a trade publication would look at.

Headline: Expert thoughts round table

This story is about the sign manufacturing client I mentioned in the regional news examples section, where they partnered with a US firm.

This piece is off the back of a round table I organised for the client with Insider magazine. Insider is a well-known online regional business publication in the North West of England. As it's a b2b trade magazine, it's aimed at other business owners. Insider focuses on big stories like mergers and acquisitions and the goings on among the movers and shakers in the industry.

My client wasn't a huge business, and I really want to emphasise that these PR opportunities aren't just the reserve of the big brands with the big budgets. There's room for smaller businesses to get their stories in there if they're pitched correctly.

Anyway, as I said, this was off the back of a round table and it's a quote from the client with the main points that came out of the round table.

As mentioned in the regional press examples section, the partnership story first appeared as a huge spread in the Nottingham Post, which goes to show that sometimes one story that might work locally may have the potential to feature in the trade press.

Always have a think, with any story or press release you write, whether there is a business angle you can bring to the trade media.

Headline: No headline

My client, a care home provider, was featured in Caring UK in a picture story without a headline. Caring UK is a publication aimed at the care sector. It has a peer-to-peer readership so this was for care homes and care providers.

The beauty of getting in this publication was that it was great for recruitment and it showed the client as an industry leader.

The front page coverage featured a lovely photo of a smiling lady at the launch of a new charitable foundation founded by the care home.

The launch party took place at one of the homes and residents got involved with the festivities. We also secured the attendance of a mezzo soprano, which added another newsworthy angle to the launch.

This was a story that worked locally and was pitched to the local press. If you have a business aimed at older people, it's worth seeing if the care sector trade press might be interested in your story.

Headline: Care provider launches charitable foundation

I secured some more coverage for the charitable launch story for my care home client, this time in UK Fundraising. The publication was interested in the fundraising and charitable aspect, as opposed to Caring UK, which focused on the launch party itself.

UK Fundraising wanted to know what the charitable foundation will do and what it signifies. The story focussed on how it was a new foundation and a new way of fundraising.

Again, this goes to show how one story can be used across different publications.

Headline: Sign manufacturing powers align to provide one-source global rebranding solution

This is a trade publication aimed at the signage industry. It's the same client and story that appeared in the Insider round table and the Nottingham Post in the regional media examples section.

The angle of interest for this publication was that these two big players in the signage industry had come together to make an even bigger wave in the industry.

As you can see, these are a few examples from different industries to inspire you to find the trade stories in your business.

Homework - What stories do you have that might work for the trade press? Are there any stories you've thought about for the regional and consumer media that could also work for trade publications?

Right stories – Online

The days where your only opportunity for coverage was in the national or local media have gone. With an explosion in new media such as blogs or niche websites, it's never been a better time to boost your business profile.

Two bites of the media cherry

Almost all newspapers - whether national, regional or local - have a website. This means that you can potentially get two bites of the cherry, as it's not uncommon for a story that has been successfully pitched to a newspaper to also appear in the online version.

Here's how the process tends to work...

1. You pitch a story to your local newspaper.
2. The reporter likes the story and decides to run it in the paper.
3. The reporter will write it up and put it into submission.
4. The sub editor will then decide whether to include the story in the paper. It is during this process that someone (whether it's the sub-editor or online editor) decides whether it also appears online.

I would generally say to pitch the story to the reporter rather than the online editor because, more often than not, what appears in the paper also ends up online. Of course, there are exceptions to the rule, and sometimes it's happened in reverse where a story has appeared online on the newspaper's website but it hasn't actually made the printed page. But often, my stories have appeared both in print and online, much to my clients' delight.

The benefits of online publicity

I used to have some clients that didn't see the value of online media coverage. They felt that getting their story on a website didn't have the same prestige as being in a newspaper or magazine. You might feel the same. However, the benefits of having your business feature online are manifold, and I'm going to detail just some of the advantages below.

The beauty of the World Wide Web is that there are so many opportunities. You can get lots of consumer and trade publicity with niche websites that weren't available in the days before the internet. Also, the lines are blurred with online media. In the previous sections I've talked about how trade media is different to local media and how local media is different to national. Online there are no such rules. Put simply, everything in print is online now, and plenty more in addition.

Another great thing is that online content lives on forever (unless, of course, the publication folds or the website shuts down) so it's got the longevity that the print press can't offer.

Online media can expose your business to a wider audience. The clue is in the name, with it being the World Wide Web, there are so many more options for people to access it as opposed to being just in a print publication. If you get into the online version of a local newspaper, that website can be accessed anywhere from across the world. This is particularly helpful if your audience is online or you distribute products across the globe.

Another great thing about online PR (and it's something I mentioned previously) is that there's often scope for advisory articles and Q&A's. This is usually the case in a lot of the business-to-business online publications. For example, in the UK there are websites such as Real Business and Business Advice, which are aimed at SME's and small business owners, and they need lots of quality content from experts. Even if you don't have a PR story in the traditional sense with the criteria that I've mentioned previously (i.e. a new product or service, or new research), if you've got something you can advise on as an expert in your field, you can pitch it to these niche publications.

Positioning yourself as an expert

The way to get yourself expert Q&A opportunities is quite simple - do your homework and see what kind of publications are out there in your industry. What are your peers reading? If those online outlets feature advice and guide articles, then throw your hat in the ring and drop them an email with the offer of exclusive advice in your area of expertise.

Unlike newspapers that don't often have scope for evergreen thought leadership pieces, if you've got some advice to give, there's likely an outlet where it will be heeded.

A boost in SEO

The other major advantage of online media coverage is that it really helps with SEO (search engine optimisation, which, in layman's terms, helps you be more discoverable online). Many websites (though not all, I have to add) will include a link back to your website, which helps your SEO. Even if you don't get a link back, the mention of your name will mean that you'll come up in Google searches.

This really helps with your online marketing and your credibility because not only do your peers get to see that you're in these publications, you can then promote it further by sharing the article to your own business Facebook page, your LinkedIn profile or your website.

Once the clients who were doubtful about online PR reaped the above benefits, they quickly enjoyed the credibility that came with being featured online.

Another thing I must mention is that guest blogging is great PR. Sometimes this is called content marketing, but for me it's just another form of PR. There is an abundance of blogs out there and I'm sure you know of blogs within your industry, too. They're absolutely worth an approach, to see if they accept external content. You could offer them an exclusive guest blog or article, again showcasing your expertise.

The online PR world really is your oyster.

Online examples

Below are some examples of what online stories look like.

Headline: Life was a blur - until a new laser blasted the floating specks from Karen's eyes

The first story I wanted to show you is an example of how a newspaper article gets repurposed online. It's what I mentioned before about getting two bites of the cherry when it comes to coverage. I didn't have to do anything extra when pitching this story.

It's the case study of a patient who lived with eye floaters, which interferes with your field of vision. The surgeon was my client and he had this amazing procedure, which successfully treated her floaters.

She had a heartwarming human interest story, which was strong enough to get featured in a full-page spread in the Daily Mail. The story was printed in the newspaper and they also used it online. Again, it's a great example of how you don't need to pitch an online-specific story to the local and national media because, more often than not, they will do that for you. The editor or sub-editor will transfer it online.

Headline: Airlines need to move away from traditional recruitment to tackle pilot shortage

This is a piece in an online-specific publication, HR Review. They took a standard press release (i.e. I didn't need to tailor it to be online specific). I sent the same release to the print press. The story was off the back of a survey from my former aviation client, where it emerged that there was a pilot shortage and that airlines needed to move away from traditional methods of recruitment to tackle this.

It shows how a story can be consumer-friendly enough for the local media and also be of interest to trade publications.

As the name suggests, HR Review is aimed at HR professionals and those with an interest in the HR industry. The publication has 45,000 subscribers and many more readers online so it was a great coup and goes to show how it's totally worth looking at what online outlets there are for your business, even if they're not specifically in your sector. If I'd adopted a tunnel vision approach with this client, I might have only looked at aviation trade publications. However, thinking outside the box meant I got several pieces of PR coverage with one story.

Headline: People are constantly making assumptions about my marriage because of my race

This is an example of a first person article that appeared in Metro online. Metro is a national newspaper in the UK, with an online readership of 50million.

As my book, *The Secret Diary of an Arranged Marriage*, was aimed at debunking myths around the process, I pitched a first-person piece to Metro about the assumptions I'd faced in real life before I got married.

The result was my entire 800+ word first-person article being published in the Metro, with my name and a link back to my book. They even paid a small fee upon publication, which was a nice bonus (though do note that not all publications do this). The great thing about this opportunity is that it could work for virtually any business. For example, if a health concern triggered a lifestyle business, they'd be interested in hearing the backstory/journey. As long as the first-person story in itself is strong and compelling, they'd be interested.

Headline: Halima Khatun: Good PR is about having a strong story

This is an example of where guest blogging is really useful.

I mentioned before how guest blogging can get confused with content marketing, but don't worry yourself with the terminology. Essentially, it is great PR to get yourself on a blog because it helps with your branding and authority.

Often, blogs link back to your site so it helps with SEO (search engine optimisation), meaning your website will gain greater visibility.

Blogs also provide a great way of gaining publicity when you don't have a news story. You can get featured by offering exclusive advice.

Using the old faithful example of a doggy trainer... the top five ways to get your dog to sit, or the top five ways to get your dog to respond to your gestures would be of interest to relevant niche blogs.

These blogs welcome content because they need to be constantly populated with stories to remain fresh and relevant. Quite often, if it's a blog with just one writer, they rely upon guest blogs and that's something you can use to your advantage.

I pitched this post for my own consultancy and it was about finding stories in your business. They responded with a request for a Q&A with me, and I happily obliged. It was an amazing opportunity as the questions helped me showcase my expertise as well as reinforcing my credibility as a PR consultant.

Business Advice is an online website aimed at small businesses primarily in the UK, so my blog post was perfect for them as we shared the same target audience.

It's always worth seeking out these kinds of publications (and there'll be plenty that tailor to the audience you're trying to connect with) to see if you can offer them anything of value such as advice articles and Q&A's.

With the explosion of online publications, you have more opportunities than ever before. You're no longer reliant on just your local paper or a magazine. The opportunities are endless.

Headline: Common pitfalls when relocating staff overseas - and how to avoid them

This was a piece of coverage I secured for my aviation client in an online business publication called Real Business, which is the UK's best read SME website. They've got a specific section called 'Advice and Guides.' Often publications have dedicated sections where they invite contributors, so it's absolutely key to check in with them whether they invite external editorial.

Some publications have a set of already agreed writers, while others will take your advice but you'd need to pay for the privilege. However, more often than not, these kind of publications which are reliant on lots of articles and quality content for their website, rely on external contributions. The beauty of the Real Business coverage is that they link back to your site as well as name checking you and your business. Often, such sites will also include a short bio from their contributor to add authority to the piece. This works out great as you can share the article on your LinkedIn profile, or however you choose to promote your business. That link back should generate people visiting your website, clicking on your services and products and hopefully influencing your bottom line.

Homework – think of what blog and websites you could target with stories or articles about your business.

Etiquette

We've covered a huge amount of ground and I hope it's not been too overwhelming and that you've been pausing, taking your time and taking notes.

Hopefully, you've now got a good understanding of the basic PR principles, the type of stories that make the news and how journalists work.

Now we're going to delve into how to marry *your* stories with what journalists want. However, before I jump into finding the story in your business, which is probably the bit you can't wait to dive into, I want to talk about etiquette. Trust me, it's worth taking the time to get this right.

When I was doing face-to-face PR training with business owners, many of them said: "This is all brilliant, but I don't know how to approach a journalist. How do they work? What's the etiquette? How do I find a journalist?"

That's why this section is important.

I'm going to cover two things. First, I'm going to talk to you about how to find journalist contacts (it's easier than you think) and then I'm going to share a bit of etiquette for when it comes to approaching them.

I won't go into detail about pitching and press releases because that's in a later section, where I'll cover both.

For now, I want to touch upon the very basics for when you've got a great story, so you know who to give it to and how to give it to them.

How to find a journalist

I'm going to tell you right now - you don't have to subscribe to a super expensive directory. Google is your friend.

When you look at online publications, whether they are blogs, magazines or the online version of national, regional, local or broadcast outlets, their details are displayed in the 'Contact us' section. If it's a newspaper, sometimes it's right at the bottom, in the footer of the website. Otherwise, it could be found in the menu bar at the top.

If you go to the publication you want to target and access the 'Contact us' section, you'll see a list of editorial contacts.

One thing I tend to do when approaching publications is look for the reporter, rather than the editor or chief-editor. For a big regional publication that has different reporters for the area, I look for the reporter in my target area. Reporters are a good shout as the editors have an overview of all the stories and are often too busy to answer the phone or respond to an email. If they're having a good day, they might forward your email on to a reporter to follow up. Otherwise they might just leave your story because they haven't got time to deal with it. So look for the reporters. They have their ears on the ground and are more likely to respond.

It's a very similar thing for online and trade publications, as they have their contacts listed on their website.

Another good trick is to look at the articles that are similar to the kind of story you're offering, because you'll see the name of the journalist and their contact or Twitter handle, so you could approach them with your pitch.

As you can see, there are lots of ways and means for getting journalist contacts. I would argue that this is the easy bit.

How to approach journalists

When I talk to people about PR, I find that many are scared of approaching journalists. I think it's because of all the things I mentioned earlier about them being overworked, underpaid, generally short on time and sometimes short on the phone when taking the hundredth call about a story.

Remember, it's not personal. They're just busy. However, you can make it easier for yourself (and them) by being concise and to the point with your pitch.

I'm going to teach you about pitching later on but, for now, just remember that journalists are like you and I, so don't be intimidated.

Think about it this way - if someone emailed your business with a generic sales message and you were blind copied in, you'd probably ignore it. Whereas if someone emailed you and addressed you directly by name, you're more likely to read it. So why would a journalist be any different?

A lot of people are intimidated and not sure how to approach journalists. Should they call or email? What would they say? Here's my best advice...

As a general rule, I would write your pitch down (we're going to talk about how to pitch and make it tight, etc. later on) and email it to them in the first instance. Keep it short, ideally no longer than a couple of lines, possibly followed by a press release if you have it ready.

The pitch itself is to sound the journalist out, so it'll be a simple: *This is my story (details of story). Would you be interested in hearing more?*

Now, there's a chance you won't get a reply, likely because a journalist has missed it because they're busy or it could be that it's not relevant (though after reading this book you'll start to realise what's relevant and what's not so hopefully you should have a more fine-tuned antenna) but my general rule is send that first email, give it a couple of days and if you've not heard back, pick up the phone and say: *Hi, I'm from (business name), can I run a story past you?*

It's important to ask their permission first before reeling off your story. If they say yes, you've bought yourself a couple of seconds with an interested ear. If they say it's not a good time, then you know not to bombard them with your story. Or they may not be the relevant person but they will give you the contact of their colleague. The point is, you've gone about it the right way.

The mistake people make out of nervousness is launching straight into their story and waffling on without even establishing if the reporter is:

A) The right reporter for the story.

B) Free to hear the story.

C) Interested in the story.

I've made that mistake in my early PR days. It's awkward and embarrassing. Don't do it. Don't be early days me.

Anyway, the beauty of having emailed them already a couple of days ago (which they may or may not have seen) is that you have that email in front of you, which will really help if you're a bag of nerves when pitching over the phone. That pitch will act as your script and given that the journalist is short on time and overrun with different things, you've got a tight pitch rather than getting tongue-tied on the phone and having to explain the story again.

Starting with an email helps you practice getting your pitch concise so you can reiterate over the phone if you've not heard back.

In my experience, if you've followed this advice but the story isn't for them, more often than not, the journalist will tell you why, so you'll know for next time. They might suggest what would work, what kind of things they are looking for, or even a different angle so you can rework your pitch. This information will prove invaluable. You'll have built a relationship with them, which will serve you well when pitching in the future.

In summary, Google is your friend when it comes to finding journalists. And email, then call, when it's time to pitch. With these simple steps you can't go far wrong.

Finding the story in your business

Well done for bearing with me so far. We've gone over a lot and hopefully you now have a better understanding of:

- What PR is and what it can do.
- What it means for your business.
- Where journalists come into the mix.
- How PR works.
- What kind of stories make the news.
- How YOU can harness it.

However, none of the above will work its magic for you unless you know how to apply all the learnings to your business. That's exactly what this section is about. The good news is it's not so much me waxing lyrical at you (which I know there's been a lot of up to now). Instead, there are lots of practical exercises, because to find the story in your business, I'm going to have to ask you to go look for it.

The key questions to ask yourself

We're now going to go through the key questions to ask yourself, which will be the perfect acid test to determine whether the story you're thinking of pitching is a news story or a non-story.

When going through the questions, keep in mind the publications that you want to get into. I hope by this point you've read them as I set this for an earlier homework.

Consider the following:

- What kind of stories does my target publication cover?
- What makes the news?
- Why is it news? What's the bit that's interesting, the hook that the journalist has got into?

Once you become more familiar with the way of storytelling - and I promise you, after finishing this book you will not be able to read or look at another article the same way again - you'll realise what's newsworthy and how to apply it to your business.

The key questions to ask yourself:

What's new?

- Have you got a new product to launch?
- Are you launching a new service?
- Have you taken on a new market?

- Have you expanded into a new area?
- Have you added to your range?

How new is new?

Your 'new' doesn't have to be a world first, or completely different from your existing offering. Sometimes just an iteration of your product/service is new enough. The reality is that someone has probably already done something similar to what you're doing. That's just life. Think about products on the market - the mobile phone was invented years ago but that doesn't stop the big brands from bringing out updated versions of the same phone. And they get press coverage for it, too. My point is, don't get too hung upon the newness of the new, because the danger is you might never put a story out there as you're assuming it's not newsworthy enough.

What is different?

I mentioned doggy training as a previous example. If you're a trainer, are you using a different method to other people?

Using my own example, here's what's different for my PR business:

- I'm well-versed in three different sectors - the public, private and the charity sector.
- I've seen things from both sides of the fence, having been a journalist and PR consultant.
- I'm not only doing consultancy for my clients, i.e. doing the PR for them, I'm also training small

businesses (like yours) to do their own PR.

Sometimes, you are the unique point of your business. For example, if you've got a wedding videography business and you pride yourself on going that step further and doing behind-the-scenes footage, maybe that's enough to make you stand out. Or you have specialist expertise that's unusual in your market.

What makes you stand out? Think about it for a minute.

This question is actually fundamental and something you probably asked yourself when you were setting up your business, or when you do your yearly business plan. If you didn't feel you had something great, unusual, or unique to offer, the odds are you probably wouldn't be in business. So go find your difference.

Are you bucking a trend?

Again, referring to the example of what I'm doing, most PR agencies wouldn't want to train people because it's counterintuitive. Why charge somebody once to do something at a lower fee, when you can bill them every month, charge a lot more and get that consistent income? Am I crazy? Probably. But it sure makes for a good story.

Here's another example: a cafe in London got a lot of media coverage because they served nothing but cereal. They had breakfast cereals from the 80s and 90s, providing nostalgia for diners. They were open late into the night and each bowl of cereal was expensive. As a business plan it sounds flawed. Who would want cereal at 9pm? Who would pay through the nose when they could have it at home? But it worked. It was kitsch. They got a huge amount of PR from it because it was so unusual. And in turn, the media coverage generated wider interest with people coming from all over London to eat at this cafe.

Is there a human interest angle?

I've mentioned the importance of human interest. Even if you think what you do is business focused, there may be a human interest angle.

If you're an accountant, you may think: *Well, there are hundreds of accountants. Why would I get PR? What could I offer a journalist?*

You'd be surprised. Ask yourself:

- Are you offering something more affordable for small businesses?
- Are you offering accountancy advice to single mums who want to get back into the workplace?
- Are you helping mumpreneurs who've had a career break? Are you offering something unusual and different for them?
- Is there a human interest story with it?

Sometimes, it will be your client that provides the human angle. As you saw in a previous example with the girl who had cerebral palsy, it was her story that made the news, not the doctor or hospital that provided the treatment.

To use the accountancy angle again, if, for example, you're talking about the auto-enrolment pension scheme, the human interest angle might be the importance of having a pension, and your case study might be a pensioner who is so glad they put money away each month, because now they're not relying on the state pension. That would be your human interest angle and if the pensioner was happy to share their story and be a case study, your chances of coverage are so much higher. Quite often, a journalist will say to me: "That's a really interesting story. Have you got a case study to go with it? This is because sometimes, just me saying something is brilliant won't do. They want context. They want to know how it affects the person on the street. Therefore, if you've got a case study, that's something that you can use to your advantage.

Is there a business development angle?

Are you growing as a business? You don't have to give away your turnover figures. You can talk in terms of personnel growth. If you're adding two staff members to your team of two, then you've doubled your growth!

Are you expanding into a different market? For example, are you exporting overseas?

If you've answered yes to any of the above, that is a business development and a potential story.

By reading this and asking yourself the questions, I guarantee you'll find at least one story in your business that could make a news story.

Homework - ask yourself the above questions and note down at least two answers that you think may make a good news story. You'll get a figurative shiny sticker if you can find three stories.

News story or a non-story

Okay, so we've talked a lot about the kind of questions to ask yourself, the kind of things that make the news - with real examples of coverage - and what journalists are looking for.

Now I'm going to put your knowledge to the test with a quiz called news story or non-story.

My clients in my face-to-face PR sessions love this because there's nothing like applying what you've learned, and my general view is if you can spot a news story outside of your business, you'll spot a news story in your business. You'll just know what's a good story.

Here's how it works...

I'm going to share a news headline without any context, and I want you to think whether it's a news story or a non-story based on the headline. Some are taken from real news stories featured in different publications, while others are made up.

After reading each headline, pause, take a minute and really think about whether you'd expect to see that in a publication.

Headline: Law firm voted 86th in the top 100 practices

What do you think? Is that a news story or is that a non-story?

Answer: It's a non-story. I made it up. Think about it this way, being 86th isn't very aspirational. It's not the top 10. It's not in the top 20. It's not even in the top 50. I'm sure it's a great achievement for the law firm that I made up but the reality is it's not significant enough. If it was a higher ranking number then it could possibly be a story.

Headline: Dietitian says consuming large amounts of sugar contributes to weight gain

Is that a news story or a non-story?

Answer: This is a non-story. It's a bit of a no-brainer that sugar contributes to weight gain. If it was something unusual - for example, too much exercise is counter productive as your muscles don't get a chance to rest, or that eating fruit can contribute to diabetes because of the high sugar content - then you've probably got a news story on your hands. Those are the kind of things that make you go: "Oh, that's interesting and it's not what I expected." We know sugar makes us gain weight. We know it's not good for us. We're not meant to have too many sweets or fizzy drinks, so that's really not a news story.

Headline: Middle-aged couples find family finances harder than generation before

Is that a news story or is that a non-story?

Answer: It's a news story and it was in the Financial Times' Personal Finance section. If you think about the context of this, it's relevant as the general news agenda is about the rising cost of living, the explosion of energy prices and the housing market. The golden age of pensions has gone and we're going to be working for longer, living longer and retiring later. The fact that people are saying they find it a lot harder than the generation before is relevant because it shows that we're almost going backwards when it comes to finances. It was also a very relatable story as many other people are going through the same struggles.

Headline: Survey reveals that when it comes to

recruitment, it's now a candidate's market

Is that a news story or a non-story?

Answer: It is a news story and was featured in a publication called HR Review.

Think about the headline - *It's now a candidate's market.*

If you've been job-hunting and registering with recruitment consultancies, it may seem like employers have their pick. Recruitment consultancies often take a while to get back to you or they're very difficult to get hold of (or at least that's been my experience). The general belief is that there are more candidates than jobs. To hear that it's a candidate's market, not an employer's market (i.e. the candidate has their pick of the jobs), comes as a surprise. Think back to the section on the key questions to ask yourself, where I talk about the unusual bit. That's the unusual part, which bucks the trend and challenges our general thinking.

I hope you're seeing a theme here... even if a story might seem dry on the surface, if it's something that's unusual or not what you'd expect, it might still make a news story for the right publication.

Headline: Hospital achieves 95% infection control rate

Is it a news story or is it a non-story?

Answer: It's a total non-story. You may not know this, but hospitals have to achieve a 95% infection control rate, so it's the bare minimum and therefore not a news story (though this was much to the disappointment of the hospital consultant who suggested it during one of my PR storyfinding sessions).

It's a no-brainer, really. If it's the bare minimum, why is it unusual? Also, if you go to a hospital, I think you'd expect it to be clean. In fact, it would buck the trend if it wasn't clean, but that would be a story a hospital wouldn't want publicised.

Headline: Organic skincare not just great for your skin, but socially responsible, too

Is this a news story or a non-story?

Answer: It's a news story and it was in a national paper's Style & Design section.

The story was that the company producing the skincare only employed disabled staff, which was an amazing, unusual story.

A thing to bear in mind is that journalists love a feel good angle, or a story involving a good cause. Their job is to deliver news to help people be informed and they're much happier to promote something like this than a cynical marketing ploy from a big corporate company.

Headline: Communication skills training firm launches new executive coaching program

Is that a news story or is that a non-story?

Answer: It's a news story and it was on a niche website called Digital Journal. It didn't make national news or break the internet but as a new service, it was very relevant for that publication.

Headline: Start-up workspace offers entrepreneurs 50% off

Is that a new story or is that a non-story?

Answer: It's a non-story. As it's a sale, it's more like an advert or promotional piece. If they were offering the first ten entrepreneurs a free space along with mentoring because they wanted to support start-ups, there'd be a little more meat to it, but it's a purely promotional 50% off, so that's not a news story. It's more like an advert you'd see in the newspaper, like *50% off these sofas!* or *Closing down sale!*

How did you do? I imagine some of the answers surprised you. Don't worry if you didn't get many right, as this book is yours to go over and look back at, but I hope doing something practical has helped you really apply your skills and see where your story comes in.

Press release example - Elliot for Water

I want to share with you some real examples of press releases I have worked on and their outcomes in terms of media coverage.

The first example is one I produced for a search engine called Elliot for Water. What differentiates Elliot for Water from Google is that when you click on the adverts that pop up on top of your search results, a percentage of the profits of those adverts go to water and sanitation projects in developing countries. This gives a heartwarming humanitarian aspect to their story.

The angle I used for the press release was that this search engine was empowering people to save lives at the click of a button. This was the most compelling part of the story.

We achieved local coverage in the Guardian with an article headlined: *Leighton man sets up new search engine to support world sanitation projects.*

The story also made the local TV news, as the founder was invited on to London Live off the back of the press release.

I produced two versions of the press release, making small tweaks for different mediums.

The first version was aimed at the charity and tech press. Here it is:

New search engine helps save lives with the click of a button

A brand new search engine allows internet users to make a real difference to the lives of people in desperate need of safe drinking water by simply searching the web.

Powered by Yahoo!, Elliot for Water is unlike any other search engine. While most others make money from businesses through pay-per-click (PPC), 60% of the profits made by Elliot for Water will go towards sanitation projects in developing countries.

The search engine works on the ground with local charity partners, maximizing the benefit of the project and cutting out the administration costs associated with larger charities.

The local partners implementing the projects will not take a fee from Elliot for Water but instead will benefit from the latest water purification technology from Solwa Srl, an organization that provides innovative solar-powered equipment. Solwa are supporting Elliot for Water in their unique mission.

Elliot for Water comes at a time when over 600 million people do not have access to clean water and around 2.5 billion are without adequate sanitation.

As a result, millions die each year from water-related diseases.

It is because of the water crisis that Elliot for Water was formed. The name derives from Helios, the God of the sun in ancient Greece.

Founder Andrea Demichelis, 22, says: "I set up Elliot for Water because I wanted to show people that they can make a tangible and positive impact on the world by doing something that they do every day. With Elliot for Water, helping others has never been easier. As the search engine is powered by Yahoo!, you can still enjoy the internet as you normally would but knowing that your simple searches may be saving lives.

"People can also be confident that we are working with small, local charities, so the revenue from their clicks won't get lost in larger charities which have bigger overheads, so the people that need it most are getting the maximum benefit."

Andrea and his team are planning to visit some of their partners in the new year to scope out projects to provide further reassurance to internet users. Elliot for Water will post the company's financial results on the search engine blog.

Though newly launched, Elliot for Water hopes to become the default search engine for many. Andrea concludes: "I would urge people to use Elliot for Water as they can make an impact straight away. After all, if you have the opportunity to save lives by simply searching the web wouldn't you take it?"

- Ends -

Dissecting press release

Company logo

Consider this a part of your press release template. You'd want your company logo (if you have one) at the top right of the press release template.

Then, just like a letter, you can put the date of the press release at the top left, above the headline. This will help the journalist know it's a new release.

Headline

New search engine helps save lives with the click of a button

Who wouldn't be interested in reading more? I got to the point straight away and included the touch points I mentioned in previous elements of this book. It's new. It helps save lives with the click of a button.

I had in mind that a journalist reading it would say: "*Okay, so that's what it does, but how does this work? How would a search engine save lives?*" The headline creates intrigue to hook the journalist in to want to read more.

Here's a tip when writing your press release headline...

A lot of people struggle with headlines. When I run PR courses, most attendees say that the headline is the hardest bit, as they know it has to be the main sell of the story. So a tip for getting your perfect headline is to write it last. I will usually draft the whole press release and at the end I'll come up with a headline. If you start with the headline first, it takes a lot of time, as you don't have the content written down. However, if you draft your story first, sometimes within the copy of the press release lies your headline. Or, you write the press release and then it's easier to summarise your story into one line. A headline is more likely to come to you once you've written the release and you've got your key points and narrative together.

Anyway, back to the press release...

As mentioned, this press release was aimed at the charity and tech press, so I considered them both with this title.

- A tech journalist will say: *"Okay, it's a new search engine. I'm interested."*
- A journalist for a charity publication will say: *"Oh, it saves lives with a click of a button. Let's read more."*

I'm obviously ad-libbing, but you get the gist.

Opening paragraph

A brand new search engine allows internet users to make a real difference to the lives of people in desperate need of safe drinking water by simply searching the web.

Look how short my opening paragraph is! It's just a two line sentence. It's concise yet conveys the hook of the story.

When a journalist reads the release, they want to scan it very quickly. They do not want any gems of the story to be hidden within big paragraphs. The largest paragraph in this release is five lines, and that's because it's a quote from the founder.

More detail

Powered by Yahoo!, Elliot for Water is unlike any other search engine. While most others make money from businesses through pay-per-click (PPC), 60% of the profits made by Elliot for Water will go towards sanitation projects in developing countries.

You'll see that I was careful to ensure I wasn't repeating myself. I've already said in the headline it helps save lives, now I'm dropping breadcrumbs. I'm teasing out more information, without beating around the bush. The journalist will be intrigued enough to read on, but won't feel like their time is being wasted.

When you're constructing a press release, each paragraph should add new information. It's okay to reinforce the previous points but what we don't want is repetition. If it's already been said, you don't need to repeat it.

The new information in this paragraph is that people who are in desperate need of safe drinking water will benefit from this search engine.

A journalist will still be thinking: *Okay, so how does it work? How do you translate searching the web to providing safe drinking water to a country you've never visited?*

That's when I go into more detail in this paragraph, which is still quite short at three lines.

I've set out my stall early on in the press release. The journalist knows it's about safe drinking water and now they understand the technical side of things. It's got the big, blue-sky thinking and the meat to back it up. The blue-sky thinking is in the headline, stating that this search engine will save lives with the click of a button. The first paragraph adds a little more and says it's going to help make a difference to the lives of people in desperate need of safe drinking water by searching the web. The second paragraph gives the 'how' and answers all those follow on questions.

My client said he didn't want it to be compared to Google and sound like he was taking them on. That was my first idea of a hook, but instead I said while most other search engines make money from businesses through PPC, 60% of the profits - so more than half - will go towards sanitation projects in developing countries.

I've made Elliot for Water stand out from the others. I've answered the question of what makes it different by saying *while most others make money from businesses through pay-per-click, Elliot for Water is different...* I've laid out the terms. A tech reporter will understand the PPC side of things, while a charity reporter will know about sanitation projects.

Some further context

The search engine works on the ground with local charity partners, maximizing the benefit of the project and cutting out the administration costs associated with larger charities.

This paragraph would be of particular interest to reporters who write for the third sector charity press.

You'll note that despite keeping the copy simple, there are certain terms that cannot be avoided, for example, administration costs. However, a charity reporter will be familiar with such terminology. They would use it in their writing, so I've tried to write it in the language of the journalist that will read it.

A charity reporter would think: *Okay, so local charity partners mean they're not giving it to a big umbrella international charity where there are huge admin fees, staff costs, running costs and building costs. It's cutting out the middleman so the end recipient, the person who needs the safe drinking water, will get as much benefit as possible without the money from the search engine clicks getting lost in the sea of administration that comes with larger companies.*

Reinforcing the point

The local partners implementing the projects will not take a fee from Elliot for Water but instead will benefit from the latest water purification technology from Solwa Srl, an organization that provides innovative solar-powered equipment. Solwa are supporting Elliot for Water in their unique mission.

I expand on and reinforce the story by talking more about how it's going to work. I'm reinforcing the credentials, credibility and the humanitarian aspect of the story.

The tech reporter might not be as interested in this humanitarian side. The interest for them is the fact that it's a search engine and the pay-per-click element. The charity reporter will be a lot more interested in the local partners and how they're not taking a fee so more of the profits can go to the cause.

The tie-in with Elliot for Water and Solwa, the company that provides water purification technology, adds a technical and charitable angle to the story.

Do you see what I've done here? Each sentence weaves the narrative. Each paragraph can work individually. A journalist may only have space for three paragraphs, so the top three paragraphs sufficiently convey the story. If they want to add more detail, they can talk about the local charity partners implementing the projects. However, if they don't want to or don't have space, the story can run without this extra information. These paragraphs work together beautifully but they can also work individually, too.

Explaining the need

Next, I give a little context around the need for Elliot for Water.

Elliot for Water comes at a time when over 600 million people do not have access to clean water and around 2.5 billion are without adequate sanitation. As a result, millions die each year from water-related diseases.

I've included a footnote to reference the source of the statistics, which is from water.org. This adds credibility - we're not just saying there's a problem, this is coming from a credible source.

The first four paragraphs have been all about Elliot for Water and what they're doing with a focus on the charitable element and the technology.

Paragraph five goes into why this matters on a global scale. It's a strong statement. The reason I put this here is because in order of importance, stating that it's a new search engine and explaining what it does and how there is a charitable aspect takes priority.

It's best to give the context afterwards. If I'd have put it sooner, for example, as the second paragraph straight after talking about Elliot for Water, it wouldn't have made sense because I hadn't explained what the search engine is, what it does and how it works.

The thing to bear in mind is, when it comes to PR and press releases, there really is no right or wrong answer. But there is best practice and that's what I'm teaching you to help you get the best outcome for your business. So it's not that it would be wrong to have put it higher but my advice would be to lay out what it is, then detail the why, followed by the bigger context afterwards.

The reason for the name

I was intrigued as to how the name Elliot for Water came about, therefore it made sense to include this in the press release.

It is because of the water crisis that Elliot for Water was formed. The name derives from Helios, the God of the sun in ancient Greece.

The journalist might be wondering about the reason behind the name, so I mention it here.

Client quote

Then I include a quote from the client, the founder of Elliot for Water. You're going to notice in the next section where I show you the localised release, how the founder quote is so much more important. However, here it rounds off the release as the other information took precedence.

As a basic press release etiquette, when you include a quote, you should use the full name of the person quoted and their age. If you look at a lot of business stories, it's not unusual to include the person's age. The journalist might not include this but sometimes it provides added context. For example, Mark Zuckerberg was in his early twenties when he set up Facebook and that added value to the story.

The quote is an opportunity to add opinion to the press release and make it more personal. So far, it's been factual, whereas the quote is more from the heart:

Founder Andrea Demichelis, 22, says: "I set up Elliot for Water because I wanted to show people that they can make a tangible and positive impact on the world by doing something that they do every day. With Elliot for Water, helping others has never been easier. As the search engine is powered by Yahoo!, you can still enjoy the internet as you normally would but knowing that your simple searches may be saving lives."

The founder is saying something that hasn't been said in the previous paragraphs.

He argues his case - it's next to no effort for the search engine user. You're browsing the web, which you do every day, so it's emphasising that point. You can enjoy the internet as you normally would. Nothing has to change. It's building a case - if the humanitarian aspect wasn't enough and the fact that it's on the ground with local partners, this is another thing to seal the deal. The reader will think: *It's not too much effort.*

Saying it is powered by Yahoo! adds the credibility factor. Yahoo! is a huge name, which I mentioned because a reader might have questions about the speed and usability of the search engine. With an unknown name, they may worry about it being slow and clunky but saying it is powered by Yahoo! provides reassurance.

Pushing the charitable element

"People can also be confident that we are working with small, local charities, so the revenue from their clicks won't get lost in larger charities which have bigger overheads, so the people that need it most are getting the maximum benefit."

Again, I've reinforced the point I mentioned previously about cutting out the administration costs. I put this in the quote for him (here's a secret: I write the quotes for my clients, they approve them).

When I'm putting press releases together, I'm playing devil's advocate. I'm thinking about what people will want to know and what their objections will be to using the search engine.

Why would they *not* be interested? How can we alleviate their concerns? That's the aim of his quote.

Future plans

Then I add some future plans information:

Andrea and his team are planning to visit some of their partners in the new year to scope out projects to provide further reassurance to internet users. Elliot for Water will post the company's financial results on the search engine blog.

Mentioning that they'll be putting their financial results on the search engine blog adds a further reassurance. In today's society, transparency is huge. There's a certain fatigue around big corporates squeezing out smaller businesses and perhaps not being as ethical as they should. There's a lot of noise around this in the media, too. Elliot for Water provides a refreshing change to the narrative.

As you can see, every paragraph reinforces and adds value to the last. It's all carefully thought out to really build the story.

If this seems intimidating, rest assured it's not as difficult as it looks.

I go through the questions I would ask as a reader because, don't forget, the journalist writes their article in a way that the reader will want to read it. They consider what the reader will be thinking.

Final paragraph

Though newly launched, Elliot for Water hopes to become the default search engine for many. Andrea concludes: "I would urge people to use Elliot for Water as they can make an impact straight away. After all, if you have the opportunity to save lives by simply searching the web wouldn't you take it?"

The final paragraph is a strong call-to-action. It's basically saying: *"Okay, you've read all about it, now I really hope that you start using it."*

The final quote just re-emphasises the point.

It's also the least important part of the press release. As mentioned previously, it's crucial to get the most important information at the top so that if the journalist ends up cutting it away because they've not got enough space, that wouldn't be the end of the world.

Yes, it's a call-to-action quote but if you think about it, the whole press release has been calling people to use the search engine.

Examining the release, I hope you can see that everything is in the order it should be. The fact that Andrea and his team are planning to visit some of their partners in the new year is just context. If the journalist cut that bit of information, it wouldn't be a major problem. However, the fact that it's powered by Yahoo! and is unlike any other search engine that makes money through PPC, is a vital part of the story. As is the bit about people's lives being saved by searching the web. That's your story, so you wouldn't dream of putting it at the bottom of the press release.

Ends

It sounds really straightforward and almost patronising but the journalist needs to see the end point. It's basic etiquette with a press release to write - Ends - so they know that the rest of the information underneath is just company information and further context.

Underneath you can put: *For an interview or further information contact* (followed by your email address).

Other things to include after the end:

- Company information such as when you launched.
- Your mission statement.
- Some notable achievements/award wins.

The information at the end can stay the same for every press release.

Tailoring to the local press

The above press release was aimed at the tech and the charity sector. Now I'm going to show you what we did for the local press. This press release was based on the same story of the same launch of the same search engine but as I'm going to show you, it's been angled for the local media, specifically London, where the client is from.

As I've shown previously, a local person done good is always a great news story.

You'll see that a lot of the press release remains unchanged but I've made it relevant to London.

London entrepreneur launches search engine to help save lives with the click of a button

An entrepreneur from Leighton has set up a brand new search engine, which allows internet users to make a real difference to the lives of people in desperate need of safe drinking water by simply searching the web.

Andrea Demichelis, 22, has launched Elliot for Water, a search engine which empowers people to change the lives of people across the world by simply browsing the web.

Powered by Yahoo!, Elliot for Water is unlike any other search engine. Whilst most others make money from businesses through pay-per-click (PPC), sixty percent of the profits made by Elliot for Water will go towards sanitation projects in developing countries.

The search engine works on the ground with local charity partners, maximising the benefit of the project and cutting out the administration costs associated with larger charities.

The local partners implementing the projects will not take a fee from Elliot for Water but instead will benefit from the latest water purification technology from Solwa Srl, an organization that provides innovative solar-powered equipment. Solwa are supporting Elliot for Water in their unique mission.

Elliot for Water comes at a time when over 600 million people do not have access to clean water and around 2.5 billion are without adequate sanitation. As a result, millions die each year from water-related diseases.

It is because of the water crisis that Elliot for Water was formed. The name derives from Helios, the God of the sun in ancient Greece.

"I set up Elliot for Water because I wanted to show people that they can make a tangible and positive impact on the world by doing something that they do every day. With Elliot for Water, helping others has never been easier. As the search engine is powered by Yahoo!, you can still enjoy the internet as you normally would but knowing that your simple searches may be saving lives.

"People can also be confident that we are working with small, local charities, so the revenue from their clicks won't get lost in larger charities which have bigger overheads, so the people that need it most are getting the maximum benefit."

Andrea and his team are planning to visit some of their partners in the new year to scope out projects to provide further reassurance to internet users. Elliot for Water will post the company's financial results on the search engine blog.

Though newly launched, Elliot for Water hopes to become the default search engine for many. Andrea concludes: "I would urge people to use Elliot for Water as they can make an impact straight away. After all, if you have the opportunity to save lives by simply searching the web wouldn't you take it?"

- Ends -

Dissecting the local release

Title

London entrepreneur launches search engine to help save lives with the click of a button

Compare this to the previous headline, which was aimed at the charity and tech media, where it read:

New search engine helps users save lives at the click of a button

You see? Not much has changed. I've just made it about him and his location. The London entrepreneur is launching a search engine. If you're a journalist covering a London publication, it'll get your interest.

First paragraph

An entrepreneur from Leighton has set up a brand new search engine, which allows internet users to make a real difference to the lives of people in desperate need of safe drinking water by simply searching the web.

The first paragraph is relatively short and sweet at just three lines.

Do you see similarities with the first paragraph in the charity and tech release?

I've reinforced the fact that he's from London by stating where in the city he's from, making it less about the technology and more about him.

The charity and tech media are not too bothered about where the founder is from. They want to know what the search engine does and what it's about. Whereas the London media absolutely want to know where the founder is from and why he set this up.

It starts with: *An entrepreneur from Leighton,* which is enough for a journalist from the area to want to read on. If I hadn't put this information upfront, they may have deleted the story.

Going into the 'who'

Andrea Demichelis, 22, has launched Elliot for Water, a search engine which empowers people to change the lives of people across the world by simply browsing the web.

While his name and age went right at the bottom in the previous charity and tech release, here it's upfront. As soon as we've introduced where he's from, we talk about who he is.

Further information

The rest of the release is pretty much the same:

Powered by Yahoo!, Elliot for Water is unlike any other search engine. Whilst most others make money from businesses through pay-per-click (PPC), sixty percent of the profits made by Elliot for Water will go towards sanitation projects in developing countries.

The search engine works on the ground with local charity partners, maximising the benefit of the project and cutting out the administration costs associated with larger charities.

The local partners implementing the projects will not take a fee from Elliot for Water but instead will benefit from the latest water purification technology from Solwa Srl, an organization that provides innovative solar-powered equipment. Solwa are supporting Elliot for Water in their unique mission.

Elliot for Water comes at a time when over 600 million people do not have access to clean water and around 2.5 billion are without adequate sanitation. As a result, millions die each year from water-related diseases.

It is because of the water crisis that Elliot for Water was formed. The name derives from Helios, the God of the sun in ancient Greece.

As you can see, all of this content is the same as in the tech and charity release because all these paragraphs are still relevant to the local media. The local press still want to know what the search engine does. The 'how' question is still there and the reasoning is still necessary. However, all of this is only relevant to the local London media if the founder or the company is from there. If not, it might as well be any person from anywhere because they are only interested in local people and local businesses.

You may think it's being lazy using the same content for the local release but it's not. It's being efficient and not reinventing the wheel. The information is still applicable to the local media. If it wasn't, I wouldn't have included it or it would have been tweaked. I hope this shows you that tailoring your release to different audiences needn't be a lengthy, onerous task. Some simple changes are often enough.

Some pointers for you...

- If you have an app and have written a press release for a tech magazine and would like to share it with the local media, put your locality up in the headline and the first paragraph to localise it. Include your age, too.
- If you have a clothing line and have written a local press release, you could tweak it to include more detail about your target audience to get the interest of women's magazines.
- If you're an author with a novel coming out and you have written a local release for your area, tweak it for the area in which your novel is based (if it's different from where you live).

Hopefully, you can see how some small tweaks can really change the context and the angle of a press release and make it relevant for different types of media and get even more coverage.

Press release example: RBE

I wanted to show you another example of a press release and how I put it together.

This was for my former client, RBE, a stress specialist.

They hadn't launched a new product or service, so there weren't those tick box PR basics to rely upon.

Instead, we worked together on a call-to-action press release. I've laboured the point previously, that commenting or offering a strong call-to-action about an area within your expertise can often get you PR coverage. If you note from the media coverage examples, we didn't do too badly with this release as it cut across various sectors, featuring in HR Review and City AM online and its print equivalent.

Here's the press release...

Businesses need to address the hidden cost in their workforce

A stress specialist who has helped hundreds of people manage anxiety and dozens of businesses improve efficiency using a little known treatment is turning her attention to perhaps the most stressed workforce of all - city workers.

(Name), who runs RBE, is urging city businesses to combat habitual poor timekeeping, an under reported issue that she says is draining the U.K.'s productivity.

(Name) explains: "There's been a big focus on absenteeism, which is said to cost the UK economy 16 billion a year. We've even heard about the nine billion lost annually to staff lateness, however, this is just the tip of the iceberg. There's a hidden figure that none of us know about... the cost of employees starting late, leaving early and generally being less productive at work, much of which can be attributed to stress.

"Put simply, a happy workforce is a productive workforce but employers need to be more proactive in addressing any issues within their teams before they reach a tipping point and the consequences affect a business' bottom line."

To overcome the issue, (Name) practices the groundbreaking heart math training, which enables people to control their heart rhythms and manage day-to-day stress using tools and techniques which are ground in decades of scientific research.(Name) is one of only 75 licensed group practitioners of heart math in the UK.

Working closely with company HR departments to understand any issues within the workforce, (Name) then engages employees in a unique three-step system which looks at symptoms and patterns of stress techniques for treatment and management of emotions.

(Name) has worked with a range of businesses and individuals from sectors such as law, accounting and healthcare. Clients have reported better sleep, reduced anxiety and greater clarity, all of which have improved their work.

"Many businesses may think of stress management as a bit of fluff and an unnecessary expense or simply not their priority. This is particularly the case in the business world, where employees are conditioned to think that admitting stress is a sign of weakness. However, stress is very common in the work environment. It does affect most businesses and certainly does hurt their profit. They just don't see it."

- Ends -

Dissecting the press release

I'm going to delve deep and dissect the press release so you can see exactly how we got the coverage.

Headline

Businesses need to address the hidden cost in their workforce

The title acts as a call-to-action, which summarises what the press release is about.

It's asking businesses to address the hidden cost in their workforce. It's saying that something needs to be done urgently.

You can see the difference between this and the Elliot for Water release, where the latter was about a new search engine that would help save lives. There was a newness. It was a launch.

This story is different because this is an expert sharing her expertise.

Opening paragraph

A stress specialist who has helped hundreds of people manage anxiety and dozens of businesses improve efficiency using a little known treatment is turning her attention to perhaps the most stressed workforce of all - city workers.

This was perfect for City AM because the story was aimed at finance workers.

You'll notice we've not mentioned the location of this stress specialist. We've focused on the facts. I also did a little context building and reinforcing the expertise of the client straight away so that as a reader and as a journalist, you think: *Okay, this person is qualified to talk about this subject. She knows her stuff. She's a stress specialist who helped hundreds of people manage anxiety and dozens of businesses improve efficiency.*

I create intrigue by saying: *using a little known treatment.* That's the kind of tease that would make you wonder: *What's this little known treatment about?* Straight away you want to know more and the fact that she's turning her attention to this most stressed workforce of all - city workers - makes it of interest to the business/city press.

If you think about it, a similar call-to-action could be employed for any business. For example:

- If you're a non-fiction author writing about nutrition, you could urge people to avoid fad diets.
- As a life coach, you could urge people to find their passion in life rather than settle for the 9 to 5. You could share techniques to help people discover what they want to get out of work.
- If you're a doggy trainer, you could say you're turning your attention to families where both parents work and don't have the time required to discipline their dog. You could teach resilience techniques and tools that will stay with their pet while the owners are out at work.
- If you're a yoga instructor, you could be turning your attention to new mothers who are often stressed out just before they're about to give birth. You could be urging them to adopt breathing techniques that will not only help them de-stress, but will prove useful during labour.

Whatever your area, your press release is a way of getting your message across.

The qualifying information

Then the release focuses on my client, who runs RBE, and is urging city businesses to combat habitual poor timekeeping, an under-reported issue, that she says is draining the UK's productivity.

It's a big statement. She talks of draining the UK's productivity. It's a national issue.

Habitual poor timekeeping is interesting for the media because it taps into a national debate. We talk a lot about absenteeism but habitual poor timekeeping is not as well reported. What she is saying is certainly not new or unusual. She is talking about something that needs to be tackled by UK employers.

This is an example where you can tap into a national debate and get coverage, without actually bringing anything brand new to the table.

Then it goes on to explain her quote: *There's been a big focus on absenteeism, which is said to cost the UK economy 16 billion a year.* Again, that's a reference point and I have added a footnote at the bottom of the press release to qualify this.

"We've even heard about the nine billion lost annually to staff lateness, however, this is just the tip of the iceberg. There's a hidden figure that none of us know about... the cost of employees starting late, leaving early and generally being less productive at work, much of which can be attributed to stress."

Do you see? Straight away, she's talking about this figure and the fact that nobody knows about the hidden cost of habitual poor timekeeping because it's not monitored. The unknown element makes it a compelling topic.

Then she explains the reason why it's important to address this: *Put simply, a happy workforce is a productive workforce but employers need to be more proactive in addressing any issues within their teams before they reach a tipping point and the consequences affect a business' bottom line.*

As we know, businesses are run by money and if something is affecting their profit, then they'll take action, as that's when it becomes a concern.

My client is saying we need to address this now. Because she's a stress specialist, because she's worked with hundreds of people and dozens of businesses, she's well qualified to say this. That's what makes the difference between her saying that and me, a PR specialist who doesn't know anything about stress in the workplace, saying that.

As an expert in *your* field, you have a voice and an opportunity to pitch your expertise and write a release commenting on your specialist area and why you feel it needs to change.

Then we go on to state what the client does:

To overcome the issue, (Name) practices the groundbreaking heart math training which enables people to control their heart rhythms and manage day-to-day stress using tools and techniques which are ground in decades of scientific research. (Name) is one of only 75 licensed group practitioners of heart math in the UK.

This reinforces her credibility. We've already mentioned that she's helped hundreds of people manage anxiety and dozens of businesses improve efficiency. We're now alluding to the little known, groundbreaking heart math training. The press release teases you before giving more information.

Being one of only 75 licensed group practitioners suggests scarcity - what she does is rare and unusual.

Think about your business. What do you offer that not many others do? That's the thing you want to feed into your press release.

The detail

We follow on with: *Working closely with company HR departments to understand any issues within the workforce, (Name) then engages employees in a unique three-step system which looks at symptoms and patterns of stress techniques for treatment and management of emotions.*

This is the explanation of how the heart math works and how (Name) operates.

Then I say: *(Name) has worked with a range of businesses and individuals from sectors such as law, accounting and healthcare. Clients have reported better sleep, reduced anxiety and greater clarity, all of which have improved their work.*

This is adding further context. I'm basically saying this is what she does and how she adds value.

Finally, she concludes with a powerful call to action: *"Many businesses may think of stress management as a bit of fluff and an unnecessary expense or simply not their priority. This is particularly the case in the business world, where employees are conditioned to think that admitting stress is a sign of weakness. However, stress is very common in the work environment. It does affect most businesses and certainly does hurt their profit. They just don't see it."*

The last quote rounds off her offering beautifully. The problem with services is that they are often intangible, so people don't always understand the offering. Being a stress specialist is much the same because people don't necessarily understand what it means and results are different for every individual. That's why we put in there that clients have reported better sleep, reduced anxiety and greater clarity, all of which has improved their work. By explaining in this way, we've made the intangible tangible.

The concluding quote sits perfectly because it handles the objections of a cynical journalist and a cynical reader. You might think: *What is stress management? It's an unnecessary use of my time and an unnecessary expense. I'll just deal with stress in my own way or just ignore it and it'll go away.*

My client is acknowledging that this is the attitude of many businesses. They think of stress management as a bit of fluff. She's owned this and said she understands that this is a problem in our workforce, where culturally we think stress management is irrelevant and an unnecessary expense. She's speaking directly to the readers that are city workers saying: *"We totally understand that this is how you feel and how businesses feel, however, stress is very common and it does affect businesses and certainly does hurt their profit."*

We're saying stress management is not top priority for businesses unless it starts to cost them. That's the crux of the story - there is an issue right under their noses that isn't being talked about, but they need to start having those conversations. The subtle sales message comes in where the client is almost saying: *And by the way, I am an expert. I can help you.*

Making this release work for you

If you have a service business and perhaps you don't have a brand new or exclusive offering, this is the kind of story that can get you coverage.

As I've shown previously, it appeared in the City AM newspaper, City AM online and HR Review.

Notes to editors

Down at the bottom we have our notes to editors, which will include a call to action of how to get in touch and where to get more information.

Repurposing the story

This story is another example of one press release working for multiple media outlets. I didn't have to write different releases. The key elements of the story didn't change. I just made some minor tweaks to the top line for different publications.

I'm going to show you how the same story was tailored to the local press. See below:

Colchester businesses need to address the hidden cost in their workforce

A stress specialist from Nayland who has helped hundreds of people manage anxiety and dozens of businesses improve efficiency using a little known treatment, is turning her attention to big businesses in Colchester.

(Name), who runs RBE, is urging businesses in Colchester and Essex to combat habitual poor timekeeping, an under reported issue that she says is draining the U.K.'s productivity.

(Name) explains: "There's been a big focus on absenteeism, which is said to cost the UK economy 16 billion a year. We've even heard about the nine billion lost annually to staff lateness, however, this is just the tip of the iceberg. There's a hidden figure that none of us know about... the cost of employees starting late, leaving early and generally being less productive at work, much of which can be attributed to stress.

"Put simply, a happy workforce is a productive workforce but employers need to be more proactive in addressing any issues within their teams before they reach a tipping point and the consequences affect a business' bottom line."

To overcome the issue, (Name) practices the groundbreaking heart math training, which enables people to control their heart rhythms and manage day-to-day stress using tools and techniques which are ground in decades of scientific research. (Name) is one of only 75 licensed group practitioners of heart math in the UK.

Working closely with company HR departments to understand any issues within the workforce, (Name) then engages employees in a unique three-step system which looks at symptoms and patterns of stress techniques for treatment and management of emotions.

(Name) has worked with a range of businesses and individuals from sectors such as law, accounting and healthcare. Clients have reported better sleep, reduced anxiety and greater clarity, all of which have improved their work.

"Many businesses may think of stress management as a bit of fluff and an unnecessary expense or simply not their priority. This is particularly the case in the business world, where employees are conditioned to think that admitting stress is a sign of weakness. However, stress is very common in the work environment. It does affect most businesses and certainly does hurt their profit. They just don't see it."

- Ends –

When we localised the story, similar to the Elliot for Water example, a lot of the meat remained the same but the initial context of the story was localised.

Whereas before we said businesses need to address the hidden cost in their workforce, for the local release, the headline is tweaked to say: *Colchester businesses need to address the hidden cost in their workforce.* The client is based in Colchester, so we used her locality.

For the local release we stress that it's a local business, we say: *A stress specialist from Nayland.* A local reporter will know where Nayland is and they'll know it's near Colchester.

The sentence reads: *A stress specialist from Nayland who has helped hundreds of people manage anxiety and dozens of businesses improve efficiency using a little known treatment, is turning her attention to big businesses in Colchester.*

Whereas we said previously: *She's turning her attention to the most stressed out workforce of all - city workers*, we're now talking about big businesses in Colchester.

Do you see how exactly the same story works for a different audience?

Then we introduce the client: *(Name), who runs RBE, is urging businesses in Colchester and Essex...*

It's no longer city workers. It's businesses in Colchester and Essex. This is still credible, as (Name) does work with businesses in that area.

The local release then follows on in the same way as the release aimed at City AM, explaining the big focus on absenteeism, which is said to cost the UK economy 16 billion a year. The following paragraph about a happy workforce being a productive workforce also remains the same.

Her quote is even repurposed, with the only difference being that she talks about Colchester businesses, not city workers.

The call to action remains the same: *For an interview with (Name) or further information, please contact...*

I hope this example goes to show that once you've got the basic skills and you practice these tips, it's really easy to weave a narrative together and get a press release that will get you coverage, with the potential to reuse for different publications with minimal extra effort.

Press release 101

Congratulations on coming this far in the book and getting closer to earning column inches with credibility and money can't buy publicity.

The real learning is just beginning, because this book won't mean anything until you go out there, find stories in your business, call journalists and pitch your news. And that's what you'll be doing with the help of the upcoming sections.

I guarantee, if you get just one piece of coverage it will have paid for this book many times over. It will also help boost your reputation, increase awareness and drive sales, which is what you're here for in the first place.

To recap, we've talked about what's a news story and what's a non-story, we've explored how journalists work and how to approach them and we've even stripped it right back at the beginning and covered what PR means, because there's no shame in admitting you don't know what it is.

I hope you've taken a lot of learnings from this so far. I'm going to share a way of keeping in touch at the end because I want to know how you're doing on your journey to getting priceless publicity. As you may have guessed, I am on a mission to make PR accessible to everyone, not just the reserve of big brands with deep pockets.

Press release template

I am leaving no stone unturned with this book. You *will* become great at PRing your business if you take the learnings I've laid out for you.

Below is a press release template, which I'm going to talk you through. You can also download this press release template for yourself by signing up to **my mailing list here:** https://www.subscribepage.com/pr101sub.

I've already shown you some detailed examples of real press releases I've created and dissected them so you could see it in action but this is a go-to guide for when you're putting something together, to make sure you include the key elements.

Press release essentials:

Logo

You start with your business logo at the top right. You can paste this or insert as an image into a word document.

Release or embargo date

You should include the date of the release so the journalist knows they're not getting an old story from you.

An embargo date is simply a holding date. It's useful if you've got a story that you want to send to a lot of national journalists because you think it's a big story, but you don't want them to publish it before a certain date.

You may want to embargo for numerous reasons. One of them might be to give every journalist a fair chance. If you send it to all the journalists without an embargo, a journalist that was out of the office misses the story and then a rival publication prints it. Because it has already been published elsewhere, the journalist may treat it as old news and therefore not use it. Another reason to include an embargo date could be that you have a particular launch date and you don't want the public to know about your service or product before then.

Embargoes can work quite well because they create a sense of anticipation and an element of excitement for journalists. It also levels out the playing field for journalists to have enough time to cover the story.

However, an embargo isn't legally binding, it's just an etiquette thing which most journalists respect. On a very rare occasion, an eager journalist may overlook the embargo and release the story sooner. If so, it's up to you in terms of whether to pitch to them again, but most journalists wouldn't want to risk ruining the relationship with you or your business.

Headline

The headline should be one line only and provide the gist of what the story is, whilst also being attention-grabbing enough to get the journalist's interest.

The headline will also be in the subject line of the email you send to the journalist, so it needs to be clear that it's worth them looking at. If it's a local release, you ideally want to get the locality within the headline.

If your story is about a new launch, you want to include this in the headline.

Lead paragraph

The aim of the lead paragraph is to summarise the story, leaving enough intrigue for the journalist to read on. You should try to mix up sentence length and mention your business. You would be absolutely distraught if you didn't mention your business in the first paragraph and then the journalist only printed the first paragraph of your story. This does happen sometimes when they either get too busy to go through the whole story, or they don't have enough space in the publication. Therefore, you really want to make sure you have mentioned your business from the beginning and given it the best chance of getting name checked within the publication.

The next paragraph

Okay, so you've got the journalist's interest with your snappy title and interesting first paragraph.

The next paragraph should explain the story in more detail. This is the time to clarify anything that wasn't clear in the lead paragraph.

You saw the perfect example of this with Elliot for Water, the search engine. We used the headline and first paragraph to talk about the fact it saves lives and we said that users can simply click the button and save lives when they go on the search engine. However, this didn't really explain how it works. That's when the second paragraph had its time to shine. If you remember, we talked about the fact that it's pay-per-click, which meant when users click on adverts, 60% of profits generated would go towards water and sanitation projects. While the first paragraph answers the 'what?', the second paragraph answers the 'how?'

Comment

After you've answered the 'what?' and 'how?', it's the perfect time to include a comment from yourself or a spokesperson from your business. This will put a human voice to the story and reinforce the key points. This isn't about repeating what's been already stated, it's about trying to add opinion, passion or value to the story.

Think about it this way - the press release is written in third person as that's the general etiquette but the quote from the spokesperson adds the human element, allowing you to have more of an opinion and explain the context. It adds colour to the story.

You don't want to make the comment too long, one or two paragraphs is more than enough.

The length of a press release

A press release should ideally be one page long. Less really is more. That means you're looking at around 300-350 words. Anything longer gets too waffly and detailed and you risk losing the interest of the already-busy journalist.

The only exception to the rule (and I've got a whole section devoted to this) is case studies. A case study is usually a person who's used your product or service and has a really impassioned and interesting story. It's more about them and there are a few more paragraphs. You can afford to have a longer case study, maybe one and a half pages. As I say, the case study is the exception to the rule.

Boiler plate

I never understood this term when I first started out in PR. Put simply, it's everything that goes after the end of the press release.

It is where you can add extra information. If you've attached a picture with your press release, the boiler plate is where you'd include the caption. You might see in most newspapers they have a picture and then underneath the names of the people in the picture, or a picture of the product with a description underneath. It's general PR etiquette that you would provide the caption within the boiler plate.

This would be followed by some further information, where you'd include your contact name and role within the company, your email address and telephone number. Never assume the journalist will reply to your email. They may urgently want to give you a call, so make it as easy for them as possible and include all the contact details underneath. Give them options.

Following that, you might want to put in some context about the company that isn't part of the press release. You could include some key points such as when the business launched, the product or service you're offering, etc. This is also your chance to brag, include any awards you've won, milestones reached, anything else of note worth mentioning.

Finally, you'd add a call to action for more information.

You'll already have stated your contact details above, but you can repeat this and also add your website address underneath. Don't make the mistake of not including your website address. I had a direct link to my book included in an article in the Metro, resulting in lots of sales.

The content below the notes to editors should remain the same for every press release and case study you do. You only have to create this once so you have a ready-made template to use every time.

And there you have it, a really straightforward press release template that you can use for your business to get you some great media coverage.

Press release tips and tricks

Hopefully, by now, you've got the perfect inspiration for a story about your business.

Now it's a case of getting it into the journalist's hands.

To help you along, here are some of my key tips for press release drafting.

Keep sentences short and concise, ideally two or three lines

Think about it this way, it's what I mentioned previously about attracting the journalist's attention. They're inundated with press releases, most of which don't see the light of day as they're skimming through their inbox to clear their emails. Therefore, you want to make it as easy as possible for them to find your story and quickly establish that it's the right story for their publication.

The easiest way to do this is by keeping your copy tight and your sentences short. Avoid big, chunky paragraphs of five or six lines because that will be too much information to read through and you risk them dismissing the story straight away.

One of the key things I mention in this book is about keeping things simple. It's about being ruthless with unnecessary words and phrases.

Before going into journalism, I did my undergraduate degree in English, which was all about using elaborate phrases and complex terminology. I was writing 12,000-word dissertations. However, I had to unlearn all of this when I trained as a journalist. I had to hack my copy down and get rid of extra words, superfluous terms and descriptive text. I had to be factual and to the point.

So here's a tip - when you write your press release, go back over it with a pencil and keep hacking away and taking out anything that doesn't add to the essential elements of the story.

Get to the point

A press release should not read like a movie where you have the opening sequence and it builds up to a climax towards the end. You really have to cut to the chase. The most important information needs to go at the top and the least important at the bottom.

Here's a simple way of thinking about this...

When a journalist is told that the story's got the go-ahead and the editor asks for it to be made into a 200-word article, there's no time to be precious about it. The journalist will get their red pen and start crossing out lines from the bottom of the press release and work their way up, because their assumption is that the most important information is at the top and the least important is at the bottom. That's why the crucial information that you want to be included (the gist of the story, any business messages) has got to be right at the top. Otherwise, these key points risk being lost should the journalist cut down the copy.

Get your business name in first

From a commercial perspective, you want to put the business name in the first paragraph, without it being like a hard sell. It's got to naturally fit.

The reason it's important to have your business name in the first paragraph is because you risk it getting lost in the rest of the story. Also, when the journalist is cutting the copy down, as I mentioned previously, they may print the story without your business being mentioned if you don't put it upfront.

If they do print your business name, but it's near the end of the story, your potential customers (i.e. the readers) might not realise it's about your business.

Use a good picture

This point may be less relevant for national media because they tend to take their own pictures when they're writing up a story, but it's important for trade, local and regional media.

If you include a good picture with your press release, it increases your chances of coverage, as the journalist needs to fill their pages with pictures to go with the stories. For example, if you run a children's crèche and you have a really cute picture of the children at play, or you're an author and you have a nice picture of yourself in front of your library of books, it's more likely to get picked up.

When you're crafting your story, think about what picture you have to go with it.

If you don't send a picture and the journalist is interested, quite often they'll request one to go with the story, so bear that in mind and try to have something ready.

Also, make sure the picture is of a high resolution so can be used in print. This is not the time to send a grainy photo from Facebook.

Customise your content

I've mentioned this previously but it's worth repeating... when writing a press release, don't try to be all things to all people. Write your release with the target audience in mind, rather than tailoring to lots of different mediums.

I've given you an example previously of my client who's in aviation. They provide solutions when it comes to recruitment and HR issues for airlines and airports and cut across many areas, including:

- The general aviation industry.
- Aviation HR and recruitment providers.
- General business media.

The HR recruitment and business media aren't going to be that interested in the nuances of aviation. Likewise, the aviation media aren't going to be interested in the nuances of HR, so it makes sense to tweak the release for the different sectors, even if it's a small change. If you can tweak your story to make it more relevant to a particular publication, then it gives you a better chance of coverage rather than sending a blanket catch-all release that's trying to tailor to everyone but in fact not getting the interest of anyone.

Keep the language simple

Idiot's English is a phrase that we often use in journalism. I know it sounds rude but essentially it means that if an idiot can read and understand it, then it passes the acid test.

You've probably heard of the phrase *idiot proof* and the idea is that anybody can read it. I'm not suggesting dumbing things down and using slang but keep the language simple and avoid too many descriptive or opinionated terms because the press release has to be factual and straightforward. If, within seconds, anybody can get the gist of what the story is about, you've done a good job.

Emailing your press release

I wanted to talk about etiquette when it comes to sending your press release by email.

It sounds really straightforward but there are some small things you can do to increase the chances of a journalist reading it.

When I started out at a PR agency, I was thrown in at the deep end and nobody told me the basics. I learnt as I went along. That's why I'm determined that you know all these things to avoid getting it wrong.

Where to put the press release

Once you've crafted your press release and you're going to email it to the journalist, rather than sending it as an attached word document, copy and paste the entire contents of the press release into the body of the email. It makes it so much easier for the journalist to read. They don't like emails with attachments as they might get sent to spam, or contain a virus.

Putting your press release into the body of the email also allows you to see how it will look for the journalist. That will help you identify any paragraphs that are too chunky, too wordy or difficult to read, so you can rectify them before hitting send.

You want to make it as easy as possible for them to open your story, read your story, and want to publish your story. The less they have to click through, the better.

Put the headline in the subject line

Once you've put the press release in the body of the email, copy and paste the headline into the subject line. I always put the precursor of 'News'. If you put news, followed by a colon, they know it's a news story. Don't forget, they're wading through hundreds of emails, some of which are adverts, special offers and outright spam. By putting news upfront, they know it's a press release within the sea of emails.

How to address a journalist to get their attention

My biggest piece of advice would be about how to address the journalist. I don't mean you call them Sir or Madam, I mean how they receive the email.

If you're sending your press release to a few journalists, always put your name in the 'To:' section and blind copy the journalists so they can't see who else it has been sent to. In the past, a PR consultant or two have been named and shamed on Twitter for CCing in over 100 journalists.

Not only is it bad etiquette (there's nothing worse than a journalist seeing who else has been sent the release) but you're also revealing their emails, which is a breach of data privacy.

You might send a story to more than one journalist at a time if you've got a world first and you want to send your press release embargoed to a few different journalists. Or you have a great case study and want to give several magazines and newspapers the option of using your story.

Pictures

Don't embed a photo into the body of the email as it won't render properly so will be a very small, pixelated picture. Also, it's difficult for the journalist to copy or save it from there. Instead, send it as an attachment to the email.

Don't send large image files as that's going to destroy their inbox. Keep it under 1mb. If you're sending a story to a national journalist, don't send a picture at all. Wait for them to ask for one, as quite often they'll want to send their own photographer to get a photo.

So that's a little email etiquette for you. It's really simple but really important and could be the difference between you getting coverage or having your press release ignored.

Pitching

Now let's talk about pitching.

A pitch is where you put your story forward to a journalist very concisely.

I've mentioned the different ways of pitching - whether you do it by email or you call a journalist to share your story over the phone - but essentially the concept of the pitch remains the same. It's no more than two paragraphs of basic information explaining what your story is about. It's breadcrumb dropping, rather than giving them the whole press release, and hoping they'd be interested to hear more.

I'm going to show you a couple of examples of the kind of pitches that would be of interest to the media to help you craft yours.

The below example is a fictional pitch about the anniversary of a doggy daycare company.

The pitch is different to a press release in that you're addressing the person directly, as though you're writing a regular email. It's informal.

Pitch example 1

Hi (name of journalist)

I would like to share the news of (location) based doggy daycare, which celebrates its 10th anniversary.

In the last decade, we've trained over a thousand dogs and to celebrate this milestone, we're hosting a Crufts-style dog show with some of our beloved dogs and their owners.

Do let me know if this is of interest or if you'd like any more information.

Regards

(Name)

Dissecting the pitch

As you can see, I include the location first to make it relevant for a local publication and local journalist.

If it was aimed at the trade press, i.e. a doggy training specific publication, I wouldn't have included the location in the first sentence because that's not of relevance to them.

Then I mention the anniversary. It's significant because it's the 10th anniversary, rather than a random year.

I add a bit of context and credibility by mentioning what we've achieved in the last decade - *we've trained over a thousand dogs*. Then I say this is what we're doing to celebrate, inviting the journalists to find out more. The journalist might want me to send them pictures after the event. They may even want to attend the Crufts-style dog show.

I sign off with: *Do let me know if this is of interest.* The pitch is so basic that they need more information. That's the idea. You want to give them minimal information so they would want more, whether the 'more' is a press release or some bullet points of information.

The difference between doing a pitch and sending a press release is that rather than giving them all the information and hoping they use it, you've provided little information to see if you can get their interest.

Pitches work really well when you're dealing with a national journalist or a trade journalist with a specialist area. They're not necessarily going to use a press release word-for-word, as they want to have an exclusive story. This is where a pitch is great because it tailors your story to what they need in a couple of lines, rather than you having to write a full press release, when there is a chance they won't even take up your story.

If I were going to a regional or a local reporter with my story, I'd usually send them a press release with all the information they need. As I mentioned previously, they prefer print-ready stories, rather than chasing someone up for more information.

A pitch is also great when you're testing the water with your story and you want to see if the journalist is interested. A pitch may also save you the job of writing a press release because the journalist might come back to you and request information in bullet point format, as they just want the bare facts. Or they might want to call you to find out more information.

As you're reading this, you're likely starting on this PR journey, so a pitch can be very useful to help you test out your stories with a journalist.

Pitch example 2

Hi (journalist name),
I would like to offer the news of a joint venture for your business pages.

Two industry leaders in the world of branding and signage from the UK and US have joined forces to form (the name of the joint venture), a one-stop design, engineering, manufacturing and project management solution for businesses across the globe.

Do let me know if you need more information on this.

Regards

(Name)

Dissecting the pitch

This pitch is about a branding joint venture and it's a real pitch that I sent to a journalist for my client, which resulted in great coverage.

Let's break it down:

1. Straight away, you know it's a joint venture story.
2. I've been helpful enough to tell the journalist where it would fit, i.e. their business pages.
3. The credibility is enforced by saying *two industry leaders in the world of branding and signage*.
4. I've detailed the sector.
5. I've mentioned the international collaboration by saying it's a UK and US company.
6. I briefly explain what they're offering by saying it's a *one-stop design, engineering, manufacturing and project management solution*. It's a bit of a mouthful but the reason there was this much detail as opposed to the more straightforward doggy daycare, is because the audiences were very different. This is for the branding press and the business press, whereas the

doggy daycare was aimed at the local media, who cover a range of topics.

For this pitch, you can assume a certain amount of knowledge and that's why it's okay to say project management solution rather than going into much greater detail.

Besides that, you can see the similarities between the two pitches. They're both short and follow on with '*do let me know if you need more information on this*'.

Clearly this isn't enough information for the journalists to go off and write their own story but it's enough to entice them to want to know more. And that is the power of pitching.

Could it be simpler?

Here's an exercise that my PR course attendees love because it really helps them think about simplifying their copy, simplifying their words and tightening their press releases and pitches.

It might seem a bit like you're back to school but bear with me... the beauty of doing this is it teaches you how to use plain-speaking English, which is something we all forget from time to time. When it comes to the media, it pays to strip things back and keep things simple and in layman's terms.

This exercise is designed to help you do just that.

The bonus of doing this is it'll not just add value to your PR copy and your press releases and pitches. Once you master this skill, it will help in your marketing messages, your website updates, your email newsletters. The benefits of mastering this are endless.

Let's make a start...

Can you simplify the following statements?

I will endeavour to do my best.

Could that be made simpler at all? Is there anything that you could change to make it as straightforward as possible? Have a think and then note down your answer.

How about this...

I will try to do my best.

You see, it's not so difficult to make that statement simpler. It's a case of finding the word that really stands out as being too long, complicated or sophisticated and swapping it for something simpler. If you do that, then whenever you write a press release, you can go through it with your red pen and take out the superfluous or overly complex terms, simplify your story and increase your chances of coverage.

Do you want to go on a bicycle ride?

Do you think that could be simplified at all?

When I was in journalism school, I was confronted with the exact same phrase and was stumped. It was like the elephant in the room. But what could we shorten?

How about this: *Do you want to go on a bike ride?*

Bicycle is not really a word we use in normal speech. We tend to say: *do you want to go on a **bike** ride?* So why would it be any different in your press release? Again, it's finding the simplest layman terms.

We need to ascertain the facts of this case.

How would you simplify this phrase?

This could easily be a quote from a legal department and can be simplified in two ways:

We need to learn the facts of this case,

or

We need to understand the facts of this case.

One thing I want to mention is that this is about best practice. I'm not saying that if you use *learn* instead of *understand,* you're wrong. I'm not saying that these are the only two options available to you, either. However, the aim of this exercise is to get you to think about how it can be simplified further.

I communicated with him.

This is something you often hear... people *communicating*. But is there a way you could make it more straightforward?

You could say:

I spoke with him,

or

I emailed him.

Or whatever the method of communication is.

Again, do you see how sometimes, by default, our language is more complicated than it need be? When it comes to writing press releases and pitches, making it as straightforward as possible is exactly what you need to do.

How did you communicate with him? You may have spoken, you may have emailed or you may have called. Be literal and state how you made conversation, as that would be a better way of constructing the statement.

This is a pivotal point in our business.

Could it be made simpler?

You could try *this is a turning point in our business.*

A really good trick to help you when you're stuck on long words is to check the synonyms. When you're writing in Microsoft word, hover over the offending word and right click on synonyms. This will give you a list of all the different words that could be used instead. You'll see all these other options that you may not have thought of and it's a great way of helping you simplify your copy.

This seems to have exacerbated the situation.

Could it be made simpler?

Yes, it can. You could have said *this seems to have made the situation worse*. You don't have to replace the word with another word. It could be a completely different sentence.

Last but not least...

It's my prerogative.

What could you say that is simpler than saying *it's my prerogative*?

Quite simply, you could say:

It's my right.

Again, synonyms are your friend.

So... how did you do?

I hope you did well but don't worry if you got stuck. That's the whole point of this learning because by going through this process, you will figure out how to simplify your copy so that it not only gets you PR coverage but it actually helps you overall in your business.

The main thing is, keep practicing, look at your marketing materials, look at your website, look at any copy you write and see if there's a way you can simplify it further because it will really help improve your PR.

Case study interview - Ruth Rees

I've talked a lot about the different ways in which you can get media coverage and the kind of stories that work, but I want to emphasise how doable it is by sharing a case study of a real business owner, with no prior PR experience, who generated great coverage for her brand.

Ruth Rees, who runs Martin Rees jewellers, received one of my free guides - *How to find PR gold in your Business* - and used the learnings when engaging the local media about a story. I sat down with Ruth for a Q&A and below is the transcript:

Q: What was your experience of PR? Had you done anything before?

A: We've been trying to get little bits in the paper for several years because Martin (Ruth's husband) and I have run this business for over 30 years together and we've done reasonably well. We've written letters to the paper on some occasions when we've had a milestone, and we find that the journalists for the local paper are usually quite cooperative, especially if you can come up with something that's reasonably well constructed. Sometimes they'll come round and take photos and send a reporter to interview but I prefer to try to write a bit of a press release so they've got something they can just use as is if they're pushed for time.

Q: How do you find writing a press release?

A: I've always enjoyed writing myself. English was one of my favourite subjects at school, so I do quite enjoy it. I also have one or two books on how to write press releases. I'd say it's well worth having a go.

Q: How did you find the How to find PR Gold in your Business guide?

I really liked the guide because while I knew some of the things that would work for the media, it jogged my memory and encouraged me to reach out to the papers. We had quite an important anniversary coming up - it was our 20th year as a pawn broker - and it made me realise I must write this up as it's something that the media might use. We ended up getting a half-page spread in the local paper and it went in the online version, too.

Several customers mentioned seeing it in the paper and I'm pretty certain we got new customers off the back of the coverage. So I was very grateful for the guide and I'm sure I'll be referring back to it again to give me other ideas in the future.

I do think PR is important in this day and age. We're all trying to keep costs down. It's harder and harder to make a profit and that's where PR is far more effective than advertising.

Turbo-charging your PR with case studies

Now, I want to talk to you about case studies and how you can harness them for your business and get yourself amazing PR, as well as lots of additional benefits.

What is a case study?

A case study is a showcase of your work. It's an illustration of what you do and it demonstrates your business in a way that you wouldn't be able to by just talking about it. Think of it as a third-party endorsement. Often, case studies are real people - your clients - that have used your business.

Case studies are great because they bring your business and story to life, and journalists absolutely love them.

Here are some examples:

- If you're an accountant, your case study could be of a start-up that has benefited from your bespoke budget service.
- If you're a lawyer, a case study might be a landmark case you've worked on.
- If you're a nutritional therapist, your case study could be a client who has seen a huge improvement in their energy levels thanks to your tailored eating plan.
- If you're a personal trainer, your case study could be a client you've helped to reach their target weight.
- If you're a stress specialist, a case study could be someone you've trained to manage their anxiety in

the workplace.

If you think about it, whatever line of business you're in, whether you're dealing directly with the public or other businesses, you *will* have a case study.

Why your business needs a case study

A case study helps illustrate your product or service better than you ever could, and with greater objectivity. When you talk about your product or service, there's an obvious bias. Of course you're going to say it's great. However, a case study, such as a client or customer, is more impartial. They don't owe you anything. They don't have a stake in your business. And as they've directly benefitted from your product or service, they will highlight your offering better than you would. That's why a case study really is worth its weight in gold.

How to make the most of a case study

In my experience, the best case studies have a human interest element with a great story.

If you think back to the national media examples I shared, the music therapy session at the care home for dementia patients was a great case study of the project, but it was the residents of the home who brought the piece to life. They added a human touch to the story. Similarly, if you think about the woman who was treated for prolapse after suffering for years, it wasn't the procedure that was interesting. It was that she felt she had got her life back. She felt like she'd solved a problem that had been plaguing her for 30 years. The procedure alone, without a real person to illustrate it, wouldn't have got the same level of media coverage.

Of course, not every business will have a human interest case study. For example, if you run an architectural firm, your case study will be the project you completed. It will be the build that you created. However, you can still humanise such case studies.

If you're an interior designer, it could be that you showcase not only the beautiful property you've worked on but also the residents. The happy homeowners that have reaped the benefit of your work can add a human interest element to the story.

If you've got a building firm and your case study is a project you've worked on, the human interest or the voice to the story will be the marketing manager in the company that you're working for (or whoever is your main point of contact within the client's business).

Whatever form of case study you have, the core principle remains that the case study should be an external endorsement of your work. It's not you saying how great you are, it's somebody else saying it for you.

Journalists love a case study

Journalists love being able to humanise a story. If you can offer them a case study, it multiplies your chance of getting coverage.

The gift that keeps on giving

The case study really is the gift that keeps on giving, because you can not only use the case study for PR purposes but you can use your case study in other areas of your marketing. For example, you can:

- Include the client testimonial on your website.
- Use it in your marketing literature.
- Tweet about it.
- Put it on your social media and add social proof to your business.

The case study options aren't restricted to getting media coverage. Once you have an amazing third-party endorsement via a case study, it propels you and your business and your marketing. People will know you're brilliant at what you do, because you're not just saying it, other people are saying it for you.

When I worked in healthcare, the case studies were often patients who could vouch for the treatments we offered.

If I was to talk about my consultancy and say: *This is what I did for other businesses and it's fantastic,* a reader might be cynical. They'd expect me to say great things about my own business. Having somebody else say it (i.e. a case study) doesn't sound like a sales pitch.

Case studies are timeless

Most case studies are evergreen and they can be pitched in the future when you don't have a news story. They don't have a shelf life. They're not responding to the news agenda. They are not necessarily about something new, or breaking, or different.

Instead, they stand on their own merit without being restricted by the usual time constraints that news stories have.

For example, if you're launching a new product or service, you'd want to send the press release at the time of launch, not a month later. Or, if you were commenting on an issue that's happening right now, you'd need to move pretty quickly. Case studies don't have the same urgency.

How to get a great case study for your business

You might be reading this book and wondering how to get a case study.

The answer is easier than you think: just ask!

It's as simple as that. Remember, you don't have to magic up these case studies. They are clients of yours that you're already working with. As long as you're giving them a great service (if not, then the issue is bigger than the scope of this book) just ask them if they'd be happy to be a case study.

In all the time I've been doing PR, I've never had a client say no to being a case study. The key is how you position it to them. Any nervousness clients may have is when they think it's a bigger, scarier process than it actually is.

Imagine saying to your client: *Hey, I'd like you to be in the media. Would you be a case study for my business?*

If you don't give them any more information, they naturally might think it's a pretty full-on request. They might have visions of a national newspaper ringing them up, or turning up on their doorstep unannounced with a camera.

In reality, a case study is nothing like that. If you follow my advice, it would be a very controlled, carefully managed process.

You need to provide the assurances to your client. They need to know that you'd first interview them over the phone.

You're going to get the information needed to make a great story. You're going to write everything down and email them the case study to make sure they're happy (this bit is really important) with what you've written **before** you even send it to a journalist.

If and when they're happy, you then send the story to a journalist. If the journalist wants more information, you're then in a position of controlling the narrative and the story as you've not just given your client's contact details away. If the journalist wants pictures, you email a picture the client has consented to give you, or one you have taken yourself. Should that journalist want to send their own photographer round for photos of the client, they would do so at a time convenient for your client.

Essentially, what you're saying to your client is that they'll be doing you a huge favour and there is minimal effort on their part and there shouldn't be any surprises. When you position it that way, it's highly likely they'll be happy to help.

If you are in an industry where things are quite sensitive, for example if you're dealing in financial services, your client might not want to talk about their financial situation. Or if you're a stress specialist, your client might not want to admit to stress. However, if you don't ask the question and offer reassurances, you will never know if they're interested in being a case study or not. Quite often, business owners second-guess before even asking. They assume clients won't be interested, when actually they might be more than happy to be involved.

I carved my career in healthcare PR, where people had very personal conditions that you'd assume they wouldn't want to discuss, let alone have splashed all over the press. However, I worked on an abundance of case studies of people who are happy with their treatment. They were singing from the rooftops!

So ask, offer reassurance and explain the process in detail. Keep reinforcing the fact that it'll be very controlled and you're not going to put their contact telephone number on a press release.

A little extra help

And here's something extra, because this book is about giving you as much value and support as possible to help you get amazing media coverage for your business.

Below is a checklist to have at hand when you're talking to a case study to ensure you capture all the information needed. This checklist transcends every business imaginable, so it will be perfect for you.

1. Introduce the process

To start with, you want to make sure you've introduced the PR process and what it will involve. It's the reassurance which I previously mentioned. It will explain the reason for the questions you're going to ask.

For example, if you're a personal trainer and you've helped a client lose weight, you are going to want to get some information, such as their age, where they live, etc. If you start asking that outright, without any context, they might be like: *Whoa, that's kind of nosey!* So you need to make sure you explain the reason for your questions.

I always launch into a case study by saying: "I'm going start with some very nosey questions. I'm afraid it's what journalists are interested in."

That tends to break the ice and helps the client understand the reason behind the question. You've also already set the expectation that there's going to be some nosey questions, so when you ask them their age, they're less likely to be offended.

Information you'll want from your case study:

- Their full name
- Age
- Occupation (particularly important if they're a business case study)
- Where they live (for the local press, you'll want the street or at least the borough within their town, as readers want to be able to relate to a local person)

Story details:

Why did you enlist our services?

Even if you already know the answer, let them tell you in their own words. You'll end up with a ready-made testimonial off the back of this, which you can use for other marketing materials.

How was life before using our services?

This is the essence of your story, because this goes into not just the *why* but it really digs into how they managed before.

How are things after using our services?

That is your narrative arc. That is the question you want to ask because it gets to the root of your story. It demonstrates the positive change you've made in somebody's business or their life.

Explaining the next steps

After getting their story, explain the rest of the PR process. Tell them you're going to write up their story and send it to them to make sure they're happy with it before anyone else sees it. Ask them for a picture, because it's great to have a photo that goes with the case study. Then get their contact details for approval. If you don't have their email address, now is a good time to get it.

As you can see, getting a case study is not rocket science. It takes a little work and it might take you out of your comfort zone, particularly if you're not in the habit of asking your clients to give you testimonials.

However, it's worth its weight in PR gold. You'll not only get great coverage, you can use it on your website, your marketing and you can share it while you're networking. The possibilities are endless, so please do try and get yourself a case study because it really will help your PR and marketing efforts.

Final note

Congratulations on getting to the end of this book!

We've covered a huge amount of ground but the learning and the development and the benefit is just beginning, as this book won't mean anything until you go out there, find stories in your business, pitch to journalists and get those column inches with credibility that you truly deserve.

I hope this was useful and I hope you've taken a lot from this book. If so, I would love for you to write a review on the store from which you bought my book.

I also want to know how you're getting on and what amazing PR coverage you are securing, because nothing makes me happier than knowing that the learnings have been applied. I am on a mission to make PR accessible to everyone. If you'd like to keep in touch (and also get my free press release template), you can join my mailing list here: https://www.subscribepage.com/pr101sub.

So... take what you've read, go get your stories out there, and I hope to see you in the media very soon.

Was this book helpful? If so, please leave a review!

Thank you again for taking the time to read my book. It makes my heart happy knowing that I am helping others with my teachings. It motivates me to write more. I want my book to be read as far and wide as possible, and key to making this happen is having great reviews from readers like you.

Reviews are the most powerful tool in my arsenal when it comes to getting attention for my books. I'm not represented by a global publishing house and I don't have a huge marketing team and endless budget.

But I have something better, that money can't buy – a committed and invested readership. And I rely upon this most important asset to spread the word.

If you've enjoyed this book, I would be grateful if you could spend just a few minutes leaving a review on the website of the store you bought this from. It can be as short or as long as you like.

About the Author

Halima Khatun is a former broadcast journalist turned PR consultant and author. With over a decade of industry experience working for the biggest PR agency group in Europe and the UK's leading corporates, she is well placed to teach all aspects of PR and storytelling. She also has a wealth of transferable skills, having worked in the public, private and charity sector.

Halima started creating PR courses to teach small businesses and start-ups to do their own PR on a budget. She has made it her mission to make PR accessible, not just the reserve of big brands with the big budgets.

As a passionate DIY PR advocate, Halima has been featured in the Huffington Post, Metro, Business Advice and StartupNation, as well as the London media.

Halima also writes women's fiction. Her award-winning debut novel *The Secret Diary of an Arranged Marriage*, has received widespread media coverage and was featured on the BBC, Good Housekeeping and more.